HOW TO WRITE COPY THAT SELLS

What They Say About Ray

"The Best Copywriting Teacher I Know."

"Ray Edwards is not only a master copywriter, he is the best copywriting teacher I know. Whether you are selling a product, a service, or a point-of-view, Ray's program will give you the training you need to move your prospects to buy NOW."

Michael Hyatt
New York Times Best-Selling Author
Platform: Get Noticed in a Noisy World

"Sales Went Through the Roof!"

"I first met Ray when I was still working with Tony Robbins. Hiring Ray was one of our best decisions. Every time we used Ray's copy, our sales went through the roof!"

Amy Porterfield, Creator of the ProfitLab

"This Stuff Is Gold"

"Ray is my go-to guy. He doesn't just talk the talk, he walks the walk. He has done everything he teaches. This stuff is gold!"

Jeff Goins, Author, *The Art of Work*

"Fantastic Work"

"Highest integrity, a pleasure to work with… and fantastic work. I love working with Ray."

Jeff Walker, *New York Times* Best-Selling Author of *Launch!*
Creator of *The Product Launch Formula*®

"One Sales Letter… $10 Million Dollars!"

"Ray flat-out gets results. He's written many profitable pieces of copy for us, including the sales letter brought us over $10,000,000 (million) in revenue."

Joe Barton, Founder & CEO Barton Publishing

"Took My Sales to the Next Level"

"I love Ray Edwards! I've used his amazing resources to take my sales to the next level. Somehow, he makes copywriting seem simple, and fun. Highly recommended!"

Cliff Ravenscraft, The Podcast Answer Man

"There's Nobody Better"

"Ray Edwards knows how to ethically sell. There's nobody better... so you make more sales, help more people & feel great about the impact you're having."

Stu McLaren, Co-Founder, Platform University

"Simply Put, Ray Is the Master ... All Others the Students."

"Ray is not only a master copywriter, but a passionate and prolific mentor to some of the most talented wordsmiths in modern-day marketing. Ray understands the complexities of today's entrepreneurial environment, and cares equally for the corporate CEO and solopreneur alike. This book is the quintessential guide for anyone who desires to grow their influence as well as their bottom line."

Brian A. Holmes, Founder - Strategic Influencers, LLC.
BrianHolmes.com

"Ray Gets Results with Class"

"There are relatively few copywriters who get results. Among them, Ray is part of a smaller group still: those who do it with class."

David Garfinkel, Founder, World Copywriting Institute

"Get 3 Copies"

"Grab your mouse and get 3 copies. Get one copy for yourself. One for your favorite vendor. And one for someone who still doubts that online copy is the "DNA" to accelerate business growth."

Alex Mandossian, CEO/Founder, AskAlexToday.com

"Holds Nothing Back"

"He is generous with his teachings and holds nothing back. Be sure to take advantage of the opportunity to sharpen your sword and let your genius copywriter within you come forth to make an impact on the web and in the world."

Joel Comm, *New York Times* Best-Selling Author
Twitter Power 3.0, Ka-Ching,* and *The Adsense Code

"Easy to Follow Blueprint for Success"

"The insights Ray shares in this book helped me more than double sales in my business. He is a skilled teacher, a gifted wordsmith, and a master at making the information you need accessible and applicable so you can use it to produce REAL RESULTS. If you're serious about growing your business you need to read, apply, and repeat what you'll learn in How to Write Copy That Sells every day—it's an easy to follow blueprint for success!"

Dr. Michael Hudson, Phd, Creator of the VisionSpeaker™ System

"The Best Email Copy I've Ever Seen"

"Ray Edwards is an absolutely brilliant copywriting and marketing mind, and writes some of the best email copy I've ever seen. "

Ben Settle, Publisher, Email Players Newsletter
The World's Foremost Expert on Email Copy

"A Must for Tech Entrepreneurs"

"Ray pulls back the mysterious curtain of the copywriting world for tech-focused entrepreneurs like me. If you understand tech but struggle to find customers, stop everything you are doing and read this book. The answers to your customer problems are in these pages."

Steve Kurti, PhD , TableTopInventing.com

"One of The Best Living Copywriters Today"

"The words 'Ray Edwards' and 'World Class Copywriting' have the same meaning to me. He is simply one of the best living copywriters today."

Mike Filsaime, MikeFilsaime.com

"Every Time I Give Ray Edwards Money, I Make More."

"Ray Edwards was the #1 influence on me to learn and love copywriting. I've participated in his exclusive, high-end trainings and can tell you that Ray helped me get my start as a copywriter, and what began as a side business grew so quickly that I left my C-suite job within one year. (Oh, and I made 5x my monthly day job income my first month going solo as a copywriter.) You're learning from the best."

Mike Kim, Marketing Strategist & Consultant, MikeKim.com

"Copywriting from the Heart"

"It is Ray's genuine integrity, penetrating honesty and extraordinary empathy that makes him a copy writing genius of our time. His concrete ethical and spiritual foundation has provided him with the golden key to unlock the hearts and wallets of your customers. This book is a must if you want to learn to sell from your heart"

AJ Slivinski, Author of *The Leadership Code*
UnlocktheLeadershipCode.com

"Authenticity and Ethical Copywriting Technique!"

"Ray's approach to nurturing and empowering consumers is the gold standard of leadership through sales. Ray demonstrates how pouring compassion and personal philosophy into customers is not only essential to quality service in a sale, it also makes a wonderful living! Ray Edwards is our universal marketing advocate: he teaches salespeople how to more effectively sell while showing consumers there is a path to being offered the best services and products in a morally sound way."

Jennifer Brenton, MD FACOG,
Founder, Mososery Health Service Corporation

"Superior Understanding of Human Psychology"

"Ray demonstrates a superior understanding of human psychology. He expertly shows you how you can use this understanding to share your message with your prospects and customers in a way that is meaningful for them. This is sure to help you to get your message out to more people and be more profitable online. Ray uses time-honored tactics, which are updated for the new medium of the internet. You hold a very powerful book in your hands—use it wisely."

Dr. Kenny Handelman, MD, Psychiatrist, TheADHDDoctor.com

"Ray Puts His Heart Into Every Word"

"Ray Edwards puts everything on the table when he teaches you the power of persuasive writing. He puts his heart into every word. His influence was the primary motivator that took me from the wreckage of homelessness to becoming a professional copywriter. Thank you Ray for teaching the world how to write words that sell."

Marshall Bone, Communications Strategist, MarshallBone.com

"Lightning in a Bottle"

"Ray Edwards has caught lightning in a bottle! How to Write Copy That Sells peeks behind the curtain into the future of copywriting, by guiding you, step-by-step, towards writing the most influential copy this side of Robert Collier. Masterful, elegant, and powerful—you will not be able to put it down!"

"DJ" Dave Bernstein, InterviewsForSuccess.com

"No Better Copywriter. Period."

"Ray Edwards has written marketing copy for me that was directly responsible for putting millions of dollars in my bank account. No better copywriter. Period. I can't believe he's putting his best secrets into a book, considering the fact that I pay him $30,000 to write a single promotion. Get this book. Now."

Matt Bacak, MattBacak.com

"Get This Book!"

"Ray Edwards is a man of impeccable integrity and it shines through in his copy and now in his book. In How to Write Copy That Sells, Ray takes you right to the heart of copywriting—what it is and, most especially, how to do it—with none of the verbal fog of most how-to books. Ray invites you into his inner sanctum where he opens his real-world copywriting tool kit. If you don't write your own copy Ray will show you how to get the very best work from those who write for you. If you do, How to Write Copy That Sells is sure money in your bank. What else can we say except—Get This Book!"

Judith Sherven,PhD & Jim Sniechowski, PhD,
Authors of Amazon #1 bestseller *The Heart of Marketing*

"An Instant Classic"

"Well, Ray, there goes my afternoon. I just read the first few chapters of your book and know I'm not going to get anything else done until I've finished the whole thing! I especially found the chapter on bullet writing brilliant—no one ever talks about it and it's so critical to the success of your online sales copy. Can I add your book to my classic marketing book website SFSBookstore. com? I think you've written an Instant Classic."

Bret Ridgway, SFSBookstore.com

"Easy to Follow Steps"

"I wish you had come out with your book a couple of years ago before I spent $1,497 for someone else's copywriting course. Your book grabbed my attention and showed me more real life examples than that course did! You spell it out from real experience and make it easy to follow your steps to creating online copy that sells. Thanks for writing such a great book!"

Wade Thomas, DomainCoach.com

"Don't Write Another Word Without It!"

"It's like having Ray Edwards sitting right next to you, showing you exactly how to write results-pulling sales copy. Jam-packed with step-by-step techniques and copywriting insights, Ray backs them up with example after example (even dissecting the copy of some of the world's top marketers to reveal why it works.) This book has earned a permanent spot next to my computer… Don't write another word without it!"

Lisa Suttora, LisaSuttora.com

"Definitely Over-Delivers"

"Ray is a great teacher because he is a great student—what he teaches he has sweated out beforehand. He expects a lot from himself and you benefit big time from his expectations. He definitely over-delivers on whatever he does—like this book. This book is a must-have reference for anyone doing business on the internet."

Harold C. Avila, DDS, MS, TMJagony.com

"Y-O-U Can Write Copy…Get This Book Today!"

"Y-O-U can write copy—that's the message that Ray Edwards conveys with How to Write Copy That Sells. And boy does he deliver! If you want to improve the results from your email, your ads, or your sales letter, get this book today."

Jeanette S. Cates, PhD, JeanetteCates.com

HOW TO WRITE
COPY THAT
SELLS

**The Step-By-Step System For
More Sales, to More Customers,
More Often**

RAY EDWARDS

New York

HOW TO WRITE COPY THAT SELLS
The Step-By-Step System For More Sales, to More Customers, More Often

Published in New York, New York, by Morgan James Publishing. Morgan James and The Entrepreneurial Publisher are trademarks of Morgan James, LLC. www.MorganJamesPublishing.com

The Morgan James Speakers Group can bring authors to your live event. For more information or to book an event visit The Morgan James Speakers Group at www.TheMorganJamesSpeakersGroup.com.

Shelfie

A **free** eBook edition is available with the purchase of this print book.

CLEARLY PRINT YOUR NAME ABOVE IN UPPER CASE

Instructions to claim your free eBook edition:
1. Download the Shelfie app for Android or iOS
2. Write your name in **UPPER CASE** above
3. Use the Shelfie app to submit a photo
4. Download your eBook to any device

ISBN 978-1-61448-502-5 paperback
ISBN 978-1-63047-502-4 eBook
ISBN 978-1-61448-503-2 hardcover
Library of Congress Control Number:
2015921095

Cover Design by:
Chris Treccani
www.3dogdesign.net

Interior Design by:
Bonnie Bushman
The Whole Caboodle Graphic Design

In an effort to support local communities and raise awareness and funds, Morgan James Publishing donates a percentage of all book sales for the life of each book to Habitat for Humanity Peninsula and Greater Williamsburg.

Get involved today, visit
www.MorganJamesBuilds.com

Habitat
for Humanity®
Peninsula and
Greater Williamsburg
Building Partner

To Lynn — in the end it's about S.O.U.

To Sean — a wise son makes a glad father.

Thank you God, for the most Important message ever written (John 3:16-17).

TABLE OF CONTENTS

INTRODUCTION

When it comes to marketing, there's one important element many business owners are missing. This single element is the key to more sales, more profits – and more of the success all entrepreneurs pursue.

- This is the one marketing tool that has created more multi-million dollar empires from scratch than any other.
- It's the single strategy that most people (and companies) ignore, thinking it is merely a small compartmentalized function of the business, when in fact it is the heart of the enterprise.
- And this is the one skill that can most quickly leverage an idea into income, and turn passion into profits…

This alchemical business ingredient: *copywriting*.

WHAT IS COPYWRITING?

It was a harsh winter in New York City. The year was 1904.

The wind howled outside, and rattled the windows of the tiny bar on the street-level floor of one of Manhattan's iconic skyscrapers.

A young man in a rumpled suit sat by himself, at a corner table, smoking a cigarette and drinking from a mug of cold coffee. John E. Kennedy was a neatly-dressed man, and his eyes were alert. He did not drink alcohol. He was in the bar for a different purpose. He kept glancing at the door, as if he were waiting for someone. He was.

Over a half hour earlier, Kennedy, an unknown copywriter, had scribbled a note and sent it upstairs, into the corporate offices of the glittering tower above. He had sent the note to Albert Lasker, one of the most powerful men in the advertising world at that time.

The note said, "I can tell you what advertising is. I know that you don't know."

It was brash. A bold move. And a total bluff.

Kennedy was betting the note might intrigue Lasker. Kennedy thought he had come up with a unique angle on how to define advertising, an angle he had never heard from anyone before. He smiled and tapped his cigarette on the ashtray next to his coffee mug. The note really amounted to the most daring bit of copy he had ever written. It was short. It was simple. It was copy about copywriting.

The front door of the bar swung open, and Kennedy looked up. When he saw the young man, the messenger he had paid to carry the note to Lasker's office, Kennedy smiled. It had worked. He flicked his cigarette into the coffee that had grown cold as he waited, shrugged on his coat, and put on his hat.

He was about to meet with the world's most influential ad man, Albert Lasker.

That meeting would change advertising forever.

Kennedy had no idea that Lasker had been searching for a satisfactory answer to this very question for seven years. Lasker's curiosity was sparked by the mysterious note from a total stranger, so he met with Kennedy.

In that historic meeting, Kennedy gave him a three-word definition of advertising: "Salesmanship in print."

It seems obvious now. Not so much in 1904.

It was a keen insight from the brilliant young John E. Kennedy. This meeting changed Kennedy's future—within four years, he was making well over six figures as Lasker's chief copywriter, at a time when that salary placed him squarely in the top 1% of all income-earners in the world.

Along with Kennedy's future, the nature of advertising was also forever changed. Even today, in the internet age, our marketing and selling processes are still informed by Kennedy's insight.

Advertising, and by extension copywriting (which is the writing of ads) is simply *salesmanship in print.*

In our case today, "print" can be extended to include not just paper and ink, but also web pages, videos, podcasts, social media updates, and more.

It is my proposal to you that copywriting is, in fact, the most pivotal and essential business skill you can learn.

THE WORLD'S MOST VALUABLE SKILL

There is virtually no other skill that can make you as much money as copywriting. Nearly all internet millionaires know this secret: more than their product, more than their traffic-generation techniques, more than their email campaigns, more than who their joint-venture partners might be, it's their *copywriting* that has made them rich.

The wealth secret of nearly all businesses, and especially internet-based businesses, is the secret of great copywriting. This book will teach you how to use that secret for yourself.

I have seen the power and the effectiveness of this skill first-hand. For over thirty years, I've written sales and marketing copy for hundreds of clients, including banks, real estate brokers, hair-transplant surgeons, auto dealers, insurance agents, radio stations, hot tub dealers, pet stores, furniture stores, TV stations, and high-tech firms.

I've had the privilege of writing copy and conducting marketing campaigns for Fortune 500 companies, for the largest broadcast companies in the world, and for the top names in leadership and business.

All my knowledge of the fundamentals of copywriting can be found in this book. Every piece of the puzzle I have used to make a high six-figure personal income is right here. At the end of this book, you will know all my best copywriting secrets.

Each chapter will cover a different aspect of copywriting, and how to use those skills for your online (or offline) business. The wealth of knowledge that you are holding in your hands could easily cost you tens-of-thousands of dollars if you tried to obtain it on your own. It represents an investment on my part of an estimated $250,000. That's what I have personally spent on my own education in this area. That, and decades of my life.

One of the main reasons I wrote this book is to save you that time, trouble, and expense. In other words, to save you the thirty years and the $250,000.

This book will give you the power to increase topline sales of any business, while simultaneously decreasing advertising cost. The result is increased bottom-line profits.

If you truly want to start your own business or create a second income stream, one of the first things I would recommend you learn is the basic skill of powerful copywriting.

Now, this is not some get rich quick scheme. This is a serious business skill that can provide you with a comfortable six-figure annual income for the rest of your life.

You can run your business from anywhere. You can dream up promotions and campaigns, write the copy, and put the plan into profit all in the same day.

And yes, you could retire from your present job and use your copywriting skills to build your own marketing empire, working wherever and whenever you want.

Or you can keep struggling along like most internet marketers and small business owners. That road leads to nowhere.

You don't need to learn the new "shiny object of the week system."

You don't need the latest greatest website.

You just need a skill that is valued and that has the power to give you leverage.

The skill I recommend starting with is the ability to write persuasive copy.

WARNING

The information supplied in this book is extremely powerful. It gives you the ability to literally manipulate people's thinking and actions. The ability to write good copy is one of the most powerful psychological tools of persuasion known to man. If you purchase this book, I hope you'll make the commitment to using these powerful persuasion tools only for the ultimate good of your customers. Never use these techniques to manipulate or control people to act against their own best interest.

*Claim **your FREE membership** (retail value $197) including a growing library of templates & tutorials, visit CopyThatSellsBook.com (no credit card required).*

1

HOW TO SELL
WITHOUT BEING "SALESY"

"Selling is essentially a transfer of feelings."
—Zig Ziglar

f you can write effective sales copy, you can literally write your own paycheck. There really should be no such thing as a "broke copywriter." By definition, good copywriters can create money out of thin air. But sales copy, ad campaigns, and business often *do* fail. Why does this happen?

It happens because just writing out a "sales pitch" is not enough to make your copy *effective*. In this chapter, we'll lay the groundwork for writing effective copy. Copy that *works*. Copy that *sells*.

FIRST YOU NEED TO KNOW YOUR "BIG IDEA"

We start with this: what are you selling, and how does it benefit the customer? You must distill this "big idea" down to a single, clear sentence. Clarifying and articulating your "big idea," or Copy Thesis™, is a crucial step in the selling process.

THE IMPORTANCE OF YOUR COPY THESIS™

"I have a conviction that no sermon is ready for preaching, not ready for writing out, until we can express its theme in a short, pregnant sentence as clear as a crystal. I find the getting of that sentence is the hardest, the most exacting, and the most fruitful labor in my study."

—J.H. Jowett

Yale Lectures on Preaching

You may remember from your school days that a thesis is "a proposition stated or put forward for consideration, especially one to be discussed and proved or to be maintained against objections." (Dictionary.com)

I can't think of a better way to define a sales message. The "getting of that sentence" may be hard work, and it may take time, but in the end it should always look similar to this:

Any [YOUR AUDIENCE] can [SOLVE THEIR PROBLEM] by using [YOUR PRODUCT], because [HOW IT SOLVES THE PROBLEM].

Examples of a strongly-constructed Copy Thesis:

- *Any **PARENT** can **IMPROVE THEIR CHILD'S BEHAVIOR** by using **YOUR BEST KID NOW**, because **IT MAKES GOOD BEHAVIOR AUTOMATIC.***
- *Any **BABY BOOMER** can **BUILD A BUSINESS FROM HOME** by using **THE PROFIT FROM WHAT YOU ALREADY KNOW COURSE**, because it **SHOWS YOU HOW TO TURN YOUR KNOWLEDGE INTO PROFITS.***

- *Any **OBESE PERSON** can **BECOME LEAN & FIT** by following **THE FREE FROM FAT FOREVER DIET**, because it **USES YOUR BODY'S BUILT-IN FAT-BURNING FURNACE**.*

Work on your Copy Thesis until you have a rock-solid "big idea" expressed "in a short, pregnant sentence as clear as a crystal."

COPYWRITING FAILS WHEN YOU IGNORE THESE PRINCIPLES

There are universal psychological triggers that help you sell more effectively. The problem is, the field of copywriting is strewn with misleading, manipulative, and even in some cases, malicious techniques.

You can hardly "swing a cat" without hitting a copywriter who has a "formula" for writing copy.

Some of these formulas are actually quite good. Many, however, are based on tricks of manipulation and psychology that are more than a little morally questionable.

The framework I'm going to share with you here, though, is intentionally based on universal principles that are focused on doing good, and helping people make decisions that are in their own best interest.

TO SELL MORE, P.A.S.T.O.R. YOUR CUSTOMERS

Most people associate the term "pastor" with the preacher at church. While this is certainly one way of understanding the term, the original meaning of the word "pastor" was actually "to shepherd." And what does the shepherd do? He or she cares for, feeds, and protects the flock.

Now, before we go any further, I should address the habit that some marketers have of referring to their customers as their "herd." It seems to paint an unflattering picture.

This kind of imagery is not what I am invoking here. The actual role of a shepherd is a loving, caring, and protective one. In fact, Jesus, who called himself the "good Shepherd," actually laid down his life for his flock.

I am not suggesting any religious overtones for your copy: what I am suggesting is that you adopt the same loving, caring, and protective role as you write copy for your prospects and customers.

And, as you might've guessed, P.A.S.T.O.R. is also an acronym for the major sections of your copy.

The P.A.S.T.O.R. Copywriting Framework™

"P" IS FOR PERSON, PROBLEM, AND PAIN

You must begin by identifying the *person* you are trying to reach with your message, understanding the *problem* that you are solving for them, and the *pain* that problem causes.

The simplest, most effective way to do this is to describe the problem in great detail.

It's a psychological principle identified by marketing wizard Jay Abraham: the more accurately you can describe your reader's problem in terms they relate to, the more they instinctively feel that you *must* have an answer to that problem. Use the reader's own language, the very words and phrases they use to describe the problem they want to solve.

For instance, if you are writing about fitness and weight loss, you might begin by describing their current situation this way:

You've tried every fad diet that's come along. You've started and stopped a dozen different exercise programs, perhaps joined several different gyms, but the truth is you just can't seem to take the weight off (or keep it off). Perhaps you're even feeling a little disgusted with yourself and your inability to control your eating and your weight. You feel like no matter what you try, it's not going to work.

Remember, you're not judging their behavior,; rather you are describing their experience as it currently is. This means you have to *understand* their experience as it currently is. You have to know your audience and what they are thinking.

As the great copywriting legend Robert Collier said, you have to "join the conversation that is already taking place in the reader's mind."

You must speak to the *person*, expose the *problem* you are helping solve, and make a clear connection to the *pain* the problem causes. Person, problem, pain.

As Zig Ziglar often said, "Selling is essentially a transfer of feelings."

You can't transfer something you don't have.

You must first empathize with your reader, and have the feelings they have. Then you must develop the feelings of excitement that come from knowing the problem can be solved.

> **You can't transfer something you don't have.**

Next, we need to turn up the volume on that pain.

"A" IS FOR AMPLIFY AND ASPIRATIONS

The next step is to *amplify* the consequences of not solving the problem, and the *aspirations* they hold for the future. This is really the key to making sales, and it is probably the most neglected step in the process.

What will motivate people to buy your product, invest in your service, or accept your idea is usually not the beautiful outcome framed in a positive light *on its own*. It is required rather, that before painting the picture of the "paradise" they seek, you must get them to fully experience the consequence of not solving the problem.

So while we do want to show our prospects how their life *can* look when they receive the benefits of your product, they first have to believe they *need* it. Even more important, they must *want* the solution you are offering. In other words: what does it cost them to *not* solve this problem?

Let me be clear about this: you need to place a dollar cost on this failure to solve the problem when at all possible.

You must make them aware of the cost of indecision.

When I'm writing copy about a business improvement program, for instance, I may have the reader walk through a simple exercise like this:

Write down your average monthly income over the last 12 months. Then write down what you want your average monthly income to be. Let's say that your average income is $5,000 per month, and your goal is actually to make $15,000 per month in your business. That means the gap between where you are and where you want to be is $10,000 per month. You're paying a cost of $10,000 every month you don't solve this problem.

Help your prospect see the real long-term consequences of ignoring their problem. You must make them aware of the price of indecision.

"S" IS FOR STORY, SOLUTION, AND SYSTEM

Once you have described the problem, amplified the consequences of not solving it, and painted the picture of paradise, it's time to share the story of how the problem can be solved.

This will be different depending on your situation. It might be the story of how you yourself finally solved this persistent problem. It might be the story of how you helped a client or customer discover the solution on their own.

It does need to be more than simply a description of what the solution is: telling the story of Bob, the frustrated business owner who was on the edge of bankruptcy, whose family had lost faith in him, and who, out of desperation tried one last idea that saved his business, is infinitely more powerful than simply saying, "One day, Bob figured out the answer."

Dig deeper. There is always a story to tell.

It should go without saying, but I will say it just in case: the story must absolutely be true. Don't make these things up. And if you're thinking, "But what if there is no story?" I would suggest you just haven't looked closely enough.

There is always a story to tell.

"T" IS FOR TRANSFORMATION AND TESTIMONY

Remember that whatever you're selling, whether it's a home study program, a book, a seminar, your consulting services — anything at all — what people are buying is not the "stuff," it's the *transformation*.

When people buy the *P90X* workout program, they did not wake up one morning and say to themselves, "I sure hope today somebody tries to sell me a bunch of exercise DVDs and a wall chart."

Those things (the DVD's, charts, etc.) are the *stuff*.

What buyers of *P90X* are actually *purchasing* is that lean, healthy, youthful physique they want for themselves. The *transformation*.

The delivery method (coaching, online videos, personal consultation, or product in a box) is merely the vehicle. Don't get the vehicle confused with the destination.

Don't get the vehicle confused with the destination.

It's also important that you offer testimony, real-life stories of people who have successfully made the transformation that you are providing. Study the most successful infomercials, and you'll discover that they consist of about 70% testimonials.

Most of us will not be writing infomercials, but it's important to remember there *are* three questions people are asking when you sell them coaching, consulting, or instruction about anything. The questions are:

- Has this person been able to do what they are describing for *themselves*?
- Has this person been able to teach *other people* to achieve the results they are describing?
- Will this person be *able to teach me* how to achieve these results?

Provide them with proof that the answer to all three of these questions is a resounding "Yes!"

"O" IS FOR OFFER

So far, you have defined the problem, clarified the cost of not solving it, told the story of the solution, and helped your reader visualize the transformation through testimonials from others just like themselves.

Now is the time to describe exactly what you are offering for sale.

This is the section of your copy where you lay out your offer. You can even create a subheading for the section called something clever like, "Here's Exactly What You Get."

Make certain that you focus 80% of your copy on the *transformation* itself. You *do* have to talk about the deliverables (the class schedule, the DVDs, etc.), but that should only occupy about 20% of your copy in this section.

Just remember that as you describe the deliverables in the offer section, you must keep tying them back to the transformation and benefits your buyers will receive.

So instead of simply writing that the buyer will receive "8 DVDs, each containing a 45-minute workout session," you might instead write that they will receive "8 DVDs that each contain a body-sculpting, fat-burning transformational workout that will help you craft the lean, muscular body you really want."

"R" IS FOR RESPONSE

This is one of the areas where copy tends to often be the weakest: the response request. We are *asking the customer to buy.*

At this point, you should not be shy about making this request. You should *tell* the customer exactly what to do in order to get your program, your consulting, your book, etc. You should remind them why it's important to do so.

I often write copy similar to this:

> *You're at the point of decision.*
>
> *You can either continue down the path of least resistance, the path you have already been traveling, or you can choose the road less traveled. The path of least resistance will probably result in you getting the same outcomes you've always received.*
>
> *But if you want something different to happen, if you want to change the direction of your health (or your relationships, or your finances, etc.) you're going to have to do something different. Make a new choice, and pursue your new outcome.*

And then I will write very specific, directive copy telling them exactly what to do next:

> *Click the button below, fill out the order form, and we will immediately ship your entire package to you. It will contain everything you need to get started.*

Some people shy away from strong language like this, but the fact is, if you truly believe that you have a solution that will solve a problem for people, why on earth would you not be as direct as possible in telling them how to get that solution?

In fact, aren't you doing them a disservice by *not* making the strongest case possible?

WHAT TO DO NOW

Use this framework to write (or rewrite) your current sales copy. The key to making this approach for writing sales copy successful is having the mindset of being a "pastor."

If you apply the principles of being a *shepherd* to your readers, and you follow the sequence of the P.A.S.T.O.R formula, my prediction is you will experience more sales, more profits, and happier customers… more often.

In the next chapter, I'll give you a very specific outline for writing a highly structured sales message. I'll break the structure into discreet "building blocks." The overarching structure of these "building blocks" will be formed by the *P.A.S.T.O.R. Framework*.

CHAPTER 1 QUICK SUMMARY:

The *P.A.S.T.O.R. Copywriting Framework™*

1. **Person, Problem, Pain**: Identify the person you are writing to, the problem that your product or service is intended to solve, and the pain your person is experiencing.

2. **Amplify**: Stress the consequences of what will happen if that problem isn't solved.

3. **Story and Solution**: Tell the story of someone who has solved that problem, using your solution or even a solution like yours.

4. **Transformation and Testimony**: Articulate the results that your product or service will bring, providing real-life testimonials to strengthen your case.

5. **Offer**: Describe exactly what you are offering for sale, focusing on the transformation instead of on the deliverables (the "stuff").

6. **Response**: Ask the customer to buy, with step by step instructions telling them what to do next.

---

*Claim **your FREE membership** (retail value $197) including a growing library of templates & tutorials, visit CopyThatSellsBook.com (no credit card required).*

2

THE MAGIC BUILDING BLOCKS
OF THE PERFECT SALES LETTER

*"He who has a thing to sell and goes and whispers in a well, is not
so apt to get the dollars as he who climbs a tree and hollers."*
—Author Unknown

The internet is the most revolutionary commerce tool that we've seen in our lifetime. Millions of people spending billions of dollars every day. You can start from your kitchen table, and almost instantly become a global company, simultaneously making business transactions with clients in Boston, Barcelona, and Borneo. It's easier now, more than ever, to build a business and make a comfortable, even extravagant living.

Piece of cake, right? "If you build it, they will come." But not quite. Plenty of businesses – especially online businesses – fail. Why?

Here's where most online marketers fail:

- They get **a great idea** for a product or service.
- They **plan their business** carefully.
- They **set up a website and wait** for the orders to start rolling in.

Guess what happens? *Nothing!*

Most websites are like an Old West ghost town. You can practically see tumbleweeds blowing down the streets.

What went wrong?

Nine times out of ten, they've lost sight of the fact that the single most important ingredient to their website is the *words.*

You can have the coolest spinning, flaming, flashing, morphing graphics on your site and still not sell a dime's worth of product. The reason? *Words sell.*

The most boring, black-words-on-white-background sales page will outperform a flashy, colorful site every time... *with the right words.*

The first place to employ those words is your *sales letter.* This is the primary selling point of your website. This is where most decisions to buy are made.

WHAT IS A SALES LETTER?

This term is a holdover from the previous century. It originally referred to a letter, sent by postal mail, which was intended to result in a **direct response** from the consumer (the recipient of the letter).

It's becoming more common to hear the terms "sales letter page," "sales copy," or "sales page," but "sales letter" is still used frequently. Online, they are virtually interchangeable.

The typical sales letter has fifteen basic elements or building blocks. It's a formula. The 15 blocks fit within the P.A.S.T.O.R. Framework. And if you follow the formula, you will get predictable results. You will sell stuff.

Here's an outline of the building blocks, explaining how to use them and how they fit inside the P.A.S.T.O.R. Framework

THE 15 BUILDING BLOCKS OF A SALES LETTER

These first few blocks correspond to the "P" in P.A.S.T.O.R. – the Person, Problem, and Pain.

1) Pre-head.

The pre-head is also sometimes referred to as the "eyebrow." I guess that assumes that you think of a sales letter as a face. Because it's a sentence fragment usually found at the top left of the sales letter, it may look a bit like an eyebrow. That's a stretch, but it's the closest thing to an explanation I've found that sounds reasonable.

It might look something like this: *"Attention, Pug Owners!"*

Now, if you're the owner of a dog that belongs to the pug group, that's going to grab your attention quickly.

How do I know? Because I am a proud Pug owner, and I can tell you that anytime I see something that's directed to Pug owners, it's got my attention. I want to know: *What do you have for me? Help me spend some money on my dog!*

That's how the pre-head works. It is a short sentence fragment designed to grab the reader's initial attention. It works very well regardless of what your product might be.

If you have a product that's designed to help people learn to play guitar, the pre-head could simply be: "Attention, guitar students!" Or, if you have a product that's targeted toward people learning to fly airplanes, it could be: "Attention, student pilots!" Or, if your product is for parents whose children suffer from ADHD, it could be: "Attention, parents of ADHD kids!"

You're targeting the prime prospect for your message and you're qualifying him or her. You're saying, in essence, "Do you belong to this group? If you do, this message is for you. Pay attention!"

2) Headline.

The headline is the "ad for the rest of the ad." Its job is to make the reader want to keep on reading—specifically, to get him or her to read the next sentence. That's all your headline has to do.

Studies show that you have about two seconds to grab the attention of people who are reading your copy for the first time. That's how long it's going to take them to decide whether or not they're going to keep on reading. In many cases, they're going to click the button and they'll be gone.

So you've got to do your job well in the headline and really grab their attention. An example sales letter headline:

"They All Laughed When I Sat Down at the Piano.
But When I Started to Play..."

You may wonder why I keep referring to an "ad." What exactly do I mean by "ad"? Well, the kinds of websites that we're writing are *websites that sell.* Often they're referred to as a "sales letter" website, and what that means is that it's written in letter format as if it were a letter on paper. Often it's on one long, scrolling web page.

This is the primary tool of the online direct response marketer (that's you!), because it's been proven to be the most effective tool for the purpose. I refer to that as an ad, and I also refer to an e-mail that's trying to make a sale as an ad, and I also refer to a Facebook ad as an ad. Whatever copy you're writing, for the purposes of our discussion in this book, *it is an ad.*

Each of those items that I just mentioned—the e-mail, the sales letter, Facebook ads—has a headline, so the principles apply, even though the execution may be somewhat different. You can compare this formula to just about any sales letter you encounter online, and you'll see they all follow it to the letter.

3) Deck Copy.

Some people call this the subhead, but I think that's inaccurate because we have another block (in our imaginary "stack" of building blocks) that we're going to call a subhead. So I want to distinguish that from the deck copy, which comes right underneath the headline.

The Deck Copy will be a block of type that is usually in black bold type and set apart from the rest of the text. It comes between the headline and the beginning of the letter. An example of good Deck Copy:

Revealed on this page...

- *The Crucial ADD/ADHD 'Misconception': your child isn't "deficient" in anything...*
- *The System Meltdown: Why the system (and its treatments) has been unable to awaken your child's hidden genius...*
- <u>*YOURS FREE*</u> *– Exclusive Access To a Once In a Lifetime Teaching Series:*
  I'm teaming up with 7 other expert ADD/ADHD doctors to blow the lid off this problem and show you how to unwrap the hidden gifts of ADD/ADHD in your child –and did I mention it's ALL completely FREE?"

The job of the Deck Copy is to reinforce the impact, and expand on the idea proposed in the headline. It can also be used to arouse more curiosity.

These next few blocks correspond to the "A" and the "S" in P.A.S.T.O.R. – we amplify the pain, and we tell the **story** of our **solution**.

4) Lead.

This is the very beginning of the body of the sales letter. This is the part that comes after "Dear Friend." It can be one paragraph, two, or several. Sometimes it consists of a simple "if, then" statement; sometimes it consists of a story that is intended to persuade you to think in a certain way.

The lead sets the criteria for whom the letter is intended, and what they stand to gain by reading the rest of the copy. Think of the classic lead, which goes something like this:

> *"If you've struggled to lose weight, if you've tried every diet imaginable, if you've taken every pill, if you've tried exercise routines, machines and personal coaches and you still haven't taken the weight off; then you're about to read the letter you've been waiting for all your life. Here's why..."*

That's a strong lead. Does it do what we just talked about? Does it set the criteria for the intended reader? Does it tell you what you stand to gain by reading the letter? Apparently it's going to tell you how to lose the weight even if you've tried all this other stuff that never worked.

5) Body.

This is the bulk of your text; most of your sales letter. It also contains all the other elements that we're *about* to list. You can almost look at these top four as the main elements of the letter and the remaining parts as sub-elements that fall within the body.

Before we move on with the list, let me say a word or two about how to do the research necessary to write your ad. The first thing I do is a simple Google search on your product, and also on your target market (example: search "pug" as well as "pug owner," "pug lover," "pug training," etc.). Try to form in your mind what your market is looking for and start searching for keywords that they might use. In other words, pretend you're a Pug owner looking to find something you need or want for your pooch.

Another way to do this research is to think about the generic terms used for the product category that you're working with, and take those generic terms and combine them with the word *forum*.

That's a great way to find places where people are discussing your topic online. You can just lurk, read the threads in the discussion forums, and see what people are talking about. Look for topics that keep coming up over and over again.

If you find there are webinars hosted for the market to which you're writing copy, get on those calls. Listen to the questions that are asked. If there are "real-world" seminars, go to those seminars and talk to people who are there—not about your product, but about *their problems*. Especially attend the question-and-answer sessions at real-world seminars. Listen to the questions that people are asking.

My friend Armand Morin—who has built multiple million-dollar brands online—initially built his business by attending seminars. He was at a seminar once, taking notes - but not very *many* notes. The person next to him asked, "Armand, aren't you getting much out of this?"

He said, "It's great! I'm getting a lot out of this!"

His friend said, "But you're not taking very many notes."

Armand's response: "Oh, I'm just writing down the questions that people are asking. That's how I know what products to create."

6) Subheads.

These are smaller headlines that separate the major sections of your sales letter. I refer to them as the "bucket brigade" of your copy.

In the olden days before there were automobiles and big red fire trucks, there was the bucket brigade. This was a group of people in a village or town who would run down to the river or the lake and form a line between the water and the burning building. They stood within arm's reach of one another. The person nearest the water scooped up a bucket of water and handed it to the next person in line, and it would get passed along until it reached the burning building, where the person at the end of the line dumped the bucket of water on the flames. Then the bucket would be returned to the water source to be re-filled and passed back through the line to the fire. That's how they would put the fire out.

I'd like to take credit for inventing the "bucket brigade" analogy ... but I can't. I don't know if David Garfinkel of the World Copywriting Institute is the person who invented it, but I heard it from him first.

Subheads act like your own bucket brigade. They lead your reader through the body of your copy to get the gist of your message. My good friend and copywriter Michel Fortin says there are three things that prospects who read your copy "never do at first" (notice the "at first;" it's the job of your copy to change that!).

Prospects never *read* anything at first; they never *believe* anything at first; and they never *buy* anything at first.

At first they're not going to *read* your letter... they're going to glance at your headline and decide whether you're getting any more of their attention.

If you hold their attention, then there are three things they're going to do next. They're going to "skim, scroll and scan." They *skim* through your letter and see if there's anything of interest to them. They're going to *scan* your subheads to get the gist of your story.

They're going to *scroll* down your letter as they *skim*, and they're going to *scan* it for things that they are interested in. If you can capture their attention while they're doing this, you've overcome the first thing they never do. Remember, they never *read* anything at first.

If, and only if, you've captured their attention during this process of "skim, scroll and scan" with your powerful headline and persuasive subheads, they will go back to the top of your letter and begin to read.

Second, people never *believe* anything at first. So now that they're reading, the job of your copy becomes to overcome their disbelief and skepticism and tell them the story they wanted to hear from the beginning.

I had a conversation with somebody today, talking about the difference between manipulation and persuasion. In my opinion, manipulation is using tricks to convince people to do things they didn't want to do in the first place, things that are not in their best interest. Persuasion, on the other hand, is using tactics to persuade people to do something that is in their best interest, and that they wanted to do to start with.

Think about your own experience when you're online and searching for something… perhaps a copywriting course like my own Copywriting Academy. At first, you're going to "skim, scroll and scan" the website and decide if this is for you. When you see there are some things that interest you, you stop and begin reading.

What you really want, in this scenario, is to be convinced that this copywriting course will answer your questions and provide you with the ability to make more sales.

That's what your prospects want as well. That's the difference between manipulating them and persuading them.

If you can **get past the fears that cause them to object** to doing what you ask them to do, then you can move them to the next of those three things that people never do at first.

Finally, people never *buy* anything at first, but if you've overcome the first two, overcoming the third is often just a matter of asking. The subheads serve as the bucket brigade that moves that process along.

7) *Rapport.*

What we mean by *rapport* is relationship building. People like three kinds of people: one, those who are *like themselves*; two, those *they would like to be;* and three, those who *like them back.* Those are the keys to building rapport. Rapport is building your relationship, a friendly relationship that makes a person feel understood and valued. An example of good rapport building copy, from a sales letter about a gold instruction product:

> *"If you've ever suspected — like most good golfers I know — that the best way to get really good at golf is to just figure it out yourself…*
> *you now have **proof** it's true."*

Rapport demonstrates that you know the reader's pain, that you understand his or her problems, and that you have some common experiences that you can share that proves you understand his or her pain.

Dr. Stephen Covey's book *The Seven Habits of Highly Effective People* says that one of those habits is to "seek first to understand, *then* to be understood."

That's what building rapport is all about. This should not be a manipulative process. It can be used for those purposes; however, I hope that you won't do that.

All these techniques that we discuss, these psychological tactics, are powerful motivators of human behavior. I hope you understand that when I tell you that I want you to promise to only use them for good purposes, I mean it. These very tactics that we use in writing good sales copy, persuasive sales copy, can also be used to manipulate other people to do things that are not in their best interest.

I refuse to use these tactics that way, and it is my hope that you will as well. Rapport-building is a powerful tactic for persuading certain behaviors, so use it with care.

8) *Bullet Points.*

A **bullet point** is a brief statement that identifies a single benefit offered by your product or service. It usually doesn't reveal how that benefit is derived.

What do I mean? First of all, the reason they're called bullets is because they often appear in bullet point fashion on a sales letter. That's because bullet points are extremely scannable; they're easy to read. There's lots of white space around them; they're short; they're punchy; and if you format them correctly, a reader can gather a lot of information by scanning over bullets very quickly.

Copy that converts at a high rate (i.e., makes a lot of sales) usually has a lot of bullets. Bullets are very powerful sales tools, and I'm going to urge you to use lots of them. That's why we will spend an entire chapter on writing bullets and how it's done. There are some very specific techniques that I think you're going to find very helpful.

Want an example of a great bulleted list? Here's one from a sales letter written by world-class copywriter Clayton Makepeace:

My stunningly simple secrets for closing more sales in a month than most do in a year.
  1) *You'll discover the six foundations of a powerful close.*
  2) *Seven never-fail closing themes that work for any assignment.*
  3) *Plus two closing blunders that could cost you everything at that final decisive moment.*

Now, don't you wonder what those are?

That's the purpose of a bullet point... to create that curiosity reaction that makes you think, "I've got to know what that is!" Think about your own experience buying products from websites. Have you ever bought a product because you just had to know what one specific bullet was talking about? I have!

These next two blocks, 9 and 10, correspond to the "T" in P.A.S.T.O.R. – **testimonials** (and proof).

9) Credibility.

You often see this section of a sales letter started with a subhead that says, "Who am I and why should you listen to me?" That's a classic subhead line that is often used by marketers.

It works. You must build credibility with your prospects in order for them to lower the resistance they're naturally feeling. Why do they feel this resistance?

Fear. When they're shopping online, they're afraid of giving you their credit card number. They're afraid of giving you their e-mail address, their contact information. They're afraid you're going to rip them off. One of the keys to overcoming this fear is to establish your credibility.

Establishing credibility will answer the top question that they have once they've started reading your letter and that is, "Why should I listen to what this person has to say?"

10) Testimonials.

Testimonials are third-party verification that your solution does what it claims to do. These third parties are credible people, who have used your product or service, liked it, and are willing to endorse it.

We've all seen them. We've all seen testimonials used. Most of us probably know by now that just using someone's initials in a testimonial is not as effective as using his or her full name.

The most believable testimonial is one that is done on video and obviously not done by an actor. We can all tell when a real person gives a truly heartfelt testimonial on video as opposed to when an actor or actress gives a testimonial.

So, you want to make your testimonials as believable as possible. Usually that means getting a video testimonial.

The next best thing is to get a photograph of the person, not a studio shot, but a candid shot, and include his or her full name and website address or, even better, his or her phone number. Most people won't agree to sharing their phone number publicly, and of course you must be respectful of that. But using a phone number in a testimonial is deadly effective for making sales. My clients who have used phone numbers in testimonials report that very few people actually *call* the phone number. Those who do just want to determine if it's a real person, so the calls are generally very short.

Using the phone number of someone who's giving you a testimonial really enhances the believability of that testimonial. This starts to tie a lot of the elements of a sales letter together. The testimonial enhances believability, which enhances credibility, which means people let their guard down, which means it's easier to build rapport and to get them to accept the promise of your offer. Do you see how these things begin to weave together? That's how we form the fabric of a good sales letter.

Now, if you're just starting out, of course, you may not have *any* testimonials. In this case, you could use quotes from famous people, as long as it's clear you're not implying that the famous person is personally endorsing your product. (If he or she is, good for you!)

For example, if you have a product about doing better advertising, you could include this quote from Mark Twain inside a testimonial box: "Many a small thing has been made large by the right kind of advertising."

Now, that isn't specifically about your product, but it supports your premise that advertising is important and can make a difference in your business. Besides, it's from Mark Twain! People will read that and think, "Mark Twain's a genius. This guy must know what he's talking about!"

You can also use quotes from articles in research from credible sources. If you have a quote from a story you saw on CNN, you can use that, as long as you stay inside the boundaries of fair use. You can't steal someone's copyrighted material, but you can certainly use quotations from people in authority that would be persuasive with your audience.

These next few blocks correspond to the "O" in P.A.S.T.O.R. – we are building the **offer** (which is really the transformation our product produces).

11) *Value Justification.*

This is where you start to talk about how valuable your product, service, or solution actually is to the user. You highlight the value to your offer and do it in a way that contrasts it favorably to the price. Here's a good example…

If you are selling a course that teaches people how to save at least $10,000 on their income tax, then talk about the fact that they're going to save at least $10,000 and some people will even save $14,000, or $20,000.

Then when you reveal the price of your product being $500, it contrasts very favorably with the $10,000 in savings. I mean, really, who wouldn't hand over $500 in order to get $10,000 back? Would you give me a quarter if I give you a dollar in return? That's the value proposition that you're trying to set up, or "value justification."

My goal when writing copy is to demonstrate the value to the buyer is at least 10 times the price.

12) *Risk Reversal.*

Let's review what we've accomplished so far. We've grabbed the reader's attention, built the case that we have a solution to his or her problem, brought him or her to the place of building rapport, established our credibility, showed him or her all the benefits of our product, demonstrated for him or her how it's worked for other people, and established how valuable the product could be. Now we come to the real crux of the matter: removing any sense of risk-taking that our prospect may be feeling.

The simplest form of risk reversal is simply to say you have a 100 percent money back guarantee. You're telling them, in effect, "Try the product. If it doesn't work, you get your money back, so what have you got to lose?"

Now, of course, you have a couple of things to overcome. First of all, people have heard the phrase "100% money back guarantee" so often that it has become audio wallpaper to them. It has lost a lot of its meaning because it's been used so often—it's almost a cliché.

Your job is to find a way to express the guarantee or the risk reversal in such a way that you're taking all the risk off their shoulders and putting it onto yours, so that they feel they're taking no risk at all.

For instance, perhaps you're selling e-books. Instead of just saying, "You get a 100% money back guarantee when ordering my e-book," you might write something like this:

> *"Download my e-book, read it, and if you don't like it, then just e-mail me and I'll give you all your money back. I'm taking a risk by doing this. I can't make you give the e-book back. I can't get the atoms back off your computer when you download the digital e-book, so you could just order the e-book, ask for a refund and rip me off, but I'm going to trust that you're not going to do that to me."*

In those few sentences, you've made it obvious that the risk is really all yours.

The risk is not being taken by the prospect at all. And yes, it's true, a certain percentage of people will do exactly what your copy "suggests," they *will* rip you off by downloading the e-book and immediately asking for the refund. But not most people—in my experience, most people are honest.

By describing the situation in those terms, it's really not any different than offering a 100 percent money back guarantee. It's just using language that more vividly illustrates the fact that the seller is shouldering the risk, not the buyer. By doing so, you remove one of the biggest obstacles to making the sale.

13) Bonuses.

Your bonus is a related but unexpected gift that enhances the value of your offer. I want you to think carefully about what I just said— first, it's unexpected. Those of us in the marketing world expect there's always going to be a bonus, but in "the real world," where folks are not accustomed to seeing sales letters, and certainly not accustomed to *studying* them, prospects often are surprised.

Let's say you're selling an information product, a course on how to lose thirty pounds in thirty days, and people are reading your sales letter, which says you're going to give them instruction on how to do this very remarkable thing. They notice at the bottom of the page that you're offering a bonus. It's a workbook. This workbook will give them a place to record their progress, and it's absolutely free, if they order today.

It's worth $19, but you're going to give it to them for free. Now, that's an unexpected bonus; it's related to your primary offer, and it's valuable. It increases or enhances the value of your offer. That is a good bonus. The mistake I see people making in their online sales letters is offering bonuses that are not related to the product that they're selling and that don't enhance the value of their product.

Think of the bonus as the "extra degree." Here's what I mean: it takes 212 degrees of heat to boil water. Water at 211 degrees is very hot – but it is not boiling. When water boils, the steam generated can produce electricity or power an engine that moves a train or a ship. The extra degree of heat takes *potential* and turns it into *action*.

That's the situation with the prospect reading your sales letter. If you've done all the other parts right, they're at 211 degrees and you need to find a way to get that extra degree to make that water boil; to generate steam, and to make the sale happen. Your bonus is that extra degree, that extra nudge that pushes the prospect over the edge.

These final two blocks correspond to the "R" in P.A.S.T.O.R. – we are Requesting a Response (in other words, we're asking for the sale).

14) Call to Action or "Explicit Offer."

The Explicit Offer is sometimes called "the Call to Action." We have, up until now, been building the case for the transformation our product or service produces. You may want to think of that as the *implicit* offer. The explicit offer is simply the place in the copy where we *ask for the order* and *tell the reader what to do*. You say, "Okay, these are the details of what I'm selling you, and here's what you need to do: click this button and order now," or "Order your copy now," or "Download this product immediately," or "Get instant access." However you phrase it, you're basically saying, "Okay, I've explained all the reasons why; now it's time for you to buy."

Oddly enough, this is often a place where many business owners and marketers take a step back and become shy and reclusive, not as aggressive as they should be in asking for the sale. By the way, this also happens in real-world sales—face-to-face selling. Often a salesperson will be at an appointment with a potential buyer and will go through the entire process of selling, but won't ask for the sale.

You have to ask for the sale in order to get it. I guarantee you'll lose 100 percent of the sales that you don't ask for.

15) P.S.

Don't underestimate this one.

I know it's kind of a cliché that online sales letters have five, six, or ten PS's. Don't engage in that nonsense. The research that I've seen shows that either one or three PS's seem to work best. You certainly don't need any more than that.

I usually just use one.

Here's why the PS is important: Remember that readers skim, scroll, and scan. They start at the top and scroll all the way to the bottom. Why? Because they want to know, "What is this person selling and how much is it?" and that's usually near the bottom of the page.

So, often they'll scroll all the way to the bottom, and if you put a good, properly formatted PS at the bottom, you can restate your entire proposition in one sentence. This is the place where you sum up the top benefit that your product offers. If the copy is online, supply a link to the order form. An example of a good P.S.:

> *"P.S. The time is now. Those big corporations are going to keep taking from you till you've got nothing left to give. Do you have the courage to fight back? Your chance to make all your dreams come true has arrived. Will you go for it? Will you take action? CLICK HERE TO DO IT NOW."*

...

Those are, very simply, the fifteen basic elements of a sales letter. Make sure you have all these "blocks" in your stack, and your chances of having a winning sales letter (one that makes more sales) become much greater.

---👆---

CHAPTER 2 QUICK SUMMARY:

The 15 Building Blocks of a Sales Letter

1. **Pre-Head:** Targets the prime prospect for your message and grabs his or her attention.

2. **Headline:** The "ad for the rest of the ad;" its job is to get the reader to keep reading.

3. **Deck:** Reinforces the impact of the idea proposed in the headline and arouses curiosity.

4. **Lead:** Sets the criteria of who this letter is for and what they stand to gain by reading it.

5. **Body:** The bulk of your text; it consists of all the elements below.

6. **Subheads:** Smaller headlines separating major sections; the "bucket brigade" of your copy.

7. **Rapport:** Demonstrates you know the reader, their pain and problem.

8. **Bullet Points:** Brief statements that arouse curiosity.

9. **Credibility:** Answers, "Why should I listen to this person?"

10. **Testimonials:** Third-party proof that your solution does what you claim.

11. **Value Justification:** Highlights the value of the offer & contrasts it favorably to the price.

12. **Risk Reversal:** Removes the biggest obstacle to getting an order, which is fear.

13. **Bonus:** Unexpected gift that enhances the value of your offer; the "extra degree."

14. **Explicit Offer (Call to Action):** You "ask for the order" and tell the reader what to do.

15. **P.S.:** The place to sum up the top benefit of your product for your readers.

> *Claim **your FREE membership** (retail value $197) including a growing library of templates & tutorials, visit <u>CopyThatSellsBook.com</u> (no credit card required).*

3

HOW TO WRITE HEADLINES THAT GRAB READERS BY THE EYEBALLS AND SUCK THEM INTO YOUR MESSAGE

"If you can come up with a good headline and lead, you are almost sure to have a good ad. But even the greatest copywriter can't save an ad with a poor headline."

—John Caples

If you want to write copy that sells, this chapter focuses on one of the cornerstone skills you simply must master: headlines.

Think of the headline as the "ad for the rest of the ad." To do its job, the headline must accomplish three tasks:

1. Stop the reader in their tracks. They must stop scanning through the copy on the page, and consider the headline.
2. Make a promise (either explicitly or implicitly) that interests the reader.
3. Evoke enough curiously to compel them to keep reading the ad.

In this chapter I share a simple five-part framework that will make your headlines (and thus your blog post titles, social media posts, subheads, and email subject lines) more effective.

In my work as a marketing consultant and copywriter, I see this problem all the time: great content obscured by boring titles and headlines.

A brief story: Morgan is a client who runs an executive consulting business, and she recently started a blog as a way of marketing her services. She called me to ask what she was doing wrong.

"I post lots of content, and it's helpful stuff. But nobody seems to read it. I get zero comments."

I brought up her blog on my laptop, and the first post I saw was entitled *The Dynamics of Organizational Change Management During Transitional Periods.* I read the post. She was right, it was good content. But for some reason she had crowned it with a repulsive title.

Virtually all her posts shared this flaw.

"I think I see your problem," I said. "Nobody's interested in reading an article with that title. Your title makes the post sound like a doctoral dissertation. You need a more appealing headline."

"Okay," she said, "what would you suggest?"

I thought about the movie I had watched over the weekend.

"How about something like *The Avengers Guide to Building Superhero Teams During Troubled Times?*"

It took some convincing for Morgan to believe this wasn't a bit over-the-top, but finally she took my suggestion. Is it a coincidence that later that day this particular blog post actually began to get comments from readers? I think not.

5 ESSENTIAL QUALITIES OF A COMPELLING HEADLINE

The headlines and subheads in your sales copy (and the post titles you choose for your blog and email subject lines) serve the same purpose as headlines in a newspaper or magazine. They either draw the reader in, or they push the reader away.

Here are five essential qualities of a compelling headline:

1. **Grabs Attention.** Your headline's number-one job is to grab the reader's attention. To accomplish this, your headline must either: make a claim or promise, evoke an emotional response, or stir up curiosity.

Examples
Can You Really Be Younger Next Year?
Which Of These Five Mistakes Do You Make on Your Blog?

2. **Screens and Qualifies Readers.** Choose specific words that segment out the exact "tribe" you want to reach. Headlines that apply to everyone can just as easily apply to no one.

Examples:
Why New Authors Fail, and What to Do about It
Top 10 iPad Apps For Entrepreneurs

3. **Draws Readers into the Body Copy.** Remember you're not selling your concept or proposition in the headline. You're making one sale only: the idea of reading the rest of the post.

Examples:
How to Write a Book in Seven Days
Does God Want You to Be Rich?

4. **Communicates the "Big Idea."** What is the one true benefit of your post, and how can you communicate that to your readers in a way that is meaningful to them? Put that in your headline.

Examples:
Triple Your Productivity Instantly
The Customer Is Not Always Right

5. **Establishes Credibility.** Authority is one of the most powerful ways of gaining attention. If you have an "authority card" to play, play it in the headline if possible.

Examples:
Ph.D. Psychologist Reveals Secret Of Self-Discipline
Harvard Study Shows 3 Common Traits Of Successful People

Incorporating these five principles into your headlines should bring you more traffic, and more sales. Using them on your blog will bring you more readers, and more engagement with your tribe.

5 HEADLINE TEMPLATES TO MAKE MORE SALES TODAY

How important are headlines? So important that some of the highest-paying work in the copywriting business is creating headlines for magazine covers and tabloids. Think about it. Aren't you sometimes at least tempted to pick up those magazines in the grocery store line? That's the power of a great headline at work.

That same power will attract readers to your ads and sale pages, putting more money in your bank account.

Effective headlines tend to follow a pattern. Here are five headline templates you can use that should have more people reading your blog posts, clicking your social media links, and buying your products.

1. **The "How-To" Headline.**

The key to making this particular headline work is that you need to tie it to a benefit your reader cares about (related to your content, of course). Examples:

How to Write a Blog Post Every Day
How to Land More Clients As a Freelancer

2. The "Transactional" Headline.

This headline is all about the promise. When you truly have "Wow!" level content, this headline will grab attention. Examples:

Give Me 30 Minutes And I'll Give You More Blog Traffic
Try These 5 Tactics for a Week, And Be Twice As Productive

3. The "Reason-Why" Headline.

Robert Cialdini cites the power of the word "because" in his book *Influence: The Psychology of Persuasion*. His research showed that simply adding the word "because" to a request makes it more likely you'll get what you're asking for.

Advertising copywriters have known this secret for a long time. Decades earlier, John E. Kennedy wrote a modest little book called *Reason Why Advertising*, which has become a classic in the field.

Use the power of the "reason why" in your headlines. Examples:

Why Your Blog Posts Get Ignored, And How to Fix That
7 Reasons You Should Be Using Social Media In Your Marketing

4. The "Probing Question" Headline.

With this kind of headline, you ask a question that creates an intense desire to know the answer. Be careful with these headlines. If you ask a question like "Do You Want to Know My Blogging Secret?" You might get a discouraging answer, such as, "No."

The kind of question you want to ask is one that really evokes strong curiosity, or taps into a problem you know your reader has. Examples:

Why Don't Doctors Get Sick?
Do You Wish More People Bought Your Book?

5. **The "If-Then" Headline.**

With this headline, you contrast something that's easy for your reader to do with the major benefit of your post. Examples:

If You Can Send and Receive E-mail, You Can Build a Platform

If You Can Follow a Recipe, You Can Write Better Headlines

One final piece of advice: I have found the ultimate secret to writing really *good* headlines ... is to write a lot of really *bad* ones. The point is not to stop with just one or two attempts; write lots of possible headlines for your sales copy, subject lines for your emails, and titles for your blog posts before you finally settle on one.

Using these five headline templates, you'll create more effective copy faster than ever before.

CHAPTER 3 QUICK SUMMARY:

Key Qualities of Compelling Headlines

1. **Grabs Attention**. Your headline's number-one job is to arrest the prospect's attention with a single "big idea."

2. **Screens and Qualifies Prospects.** Choose specific words that segment out the exact prospects you want to reach. Headlines that apply to everyone can just as easily apply to no one.

3. **Draws Readers into the Body Copy.** Your headline's job is to convince readers to ... keep reading.

4. **Communicates the "Big Idea."** What is the one true benefit of your offer, and how can you communicate that to your prospects? Put that into your headline.

5. **Establishes Credibility.** If you can establish some authority in your headline or pre-head, you will be far ahead of most copywriters.

5 Headline Templates to Make More Sales Today

1. The "How-To" Headline.
2. The "Transactional" Headline.
3. The "Reason-Why" Headline.
4. The "Probing Question" Headline.
5. The "If-Then" Headline.

---

*Claim **your FREE membership** (retail value $197) including a growing library of templates & tutorials, visit CopyThatSellsBook.com (no credit card required).*

4

INBOX MAGIC: HOW TO WRITE E-MAILS THAT MAKE MORE MONEY

"Make it simple. Make it memorable. Make it inviting to look at. Make it fun to read."

—Leo Burnett

Email marketing is not dead.

Despite what people say. Despite the complaints about spam. Despite the fact that people would try to convince you that it's all "happening" in social media now, that there's no need for email. That's bull-feathers!

Email is *still* the number one way to get things sold on the internet. More things are sold via email than any other method, even more than Facebook, Twitter, LinkedIn or Google Plus.

The problem is that most people are doing it wrong. If you're doing it *wrong*, then of *course* it won't work for you. So, if you've had that experience of trying to sell via email and it didn't work out, you'll probably learn things in this chapter that will change the results you get from email.

WHY IS IT THAT EMAIL STILL WORKS?

With so many new forms of communication available (think social media, messaging services, and texting, just to name a few) – why does email still work at all?

First, it's personal. Email is the number one way we communicate with our *friends*. Yes, we do texting and messaging, but if you think about it, for most of us the majority of communication we have with friends and relatives and co-workers is via email.

It's going to be that way for quite some time.

WILL IT CHANGE EVENTUALLY AND BECOME SOMETHING ELSE?

Probably, but not today… and not next week, next month, or even next year. Therefore, we need to master communicating via email.

Even if email *does* go away, the principles you'll learn here will hold true no matter what the medium.

The most powerful reason I think email works is it's very much a point and click selling medium. People see something in the email that interests them and they click on the link, which puts them in directly in front of the message we want them to see.

Used properly, email can multiply your business results. Let's begin by examining the concept of email *sequences*.

EMAIL SEQUENCES YOU NEED FOR MAXIMUM SALES

Exactly what *kinds* of emails do you need to write and send to your list? *How* do you deliver them?

The truth is, there's no *one* right answer.

There is no *one* system that fits all companies or all personas.

There's room for improvisation, room for testing and trying things that are different from what I'm recommending – or what anyone else is doing.

After you learn the fundamentals.

I *will* give you the fundamentals here, a general framework of how to think about your email marketing.

THREE CORE EMAIL TYPES

There are three core "types" of marketing emails you need to be familiar with.

1. Campaign Sequences that you send "live."

A "campaign" is a series (or *sequence*) of emails that are sent over time for one specific promotional purpose, like a product launch or promotion. "Live" simply means you're writing the emails as you go, in real time.

2. Automated Campaign Sequences.

This is where *autoresponders* come in. An autoresponder is an automated email sent without human intervention. The sequence is timed (one email per day, or one per week, etc.) and triggered when a customer takes a certain action like making a purchase, signing up for a webinar, or registering to receive your newsletter (just to name a few).

3. Broadcast "one off" emails

This is where you send an email to everybody on your list for one specific intended purpose. It's not a sequence. It's not automated and it's not a live sequence, because it's just a single email. There are times and places where this is appropriate.

Let's break this down and talk about these three categories, what they mean and how you can build them yourself.

EMAIL TYPE 1: "LIVE" CAMPAIGN SEQUENCES

Campaign sequences that are live might be used for a *product launch*.

A *product launch* is a large-scale product rollout; that probably means you're doing a big advertising campaign. You may have joint venture partners or affiliates promoting at the same time, so you're trying to achieve a certain amount of critical mass awareness of your product rollout. This can bring you a concentrated surge in sales.

All told you may write 10-20 days' worth of emails in this product launch sequence. Maybe one or two emails a day for the last few days… and it's all done "live." It's written as you go, so you can respond to questions, and to changes that happen in the marketplace. You can include references to news and TV shows, and other current events in your email that prove they're live. This kind of timely content will also match and mirror the experience and daily life of your prospects and readers. This is very powerful, because you can respond to questions and comments you get via email and surveys you may be conducting.

A *promotion* would work much the same way, but is more of a smaller-scale kind of advertising campaign that does not center around a large coordinated effort. You may be promoting an existing product or a new product, maybe a small ticket item, $47 or $97. Probably, you're just mailing to your house list. In other words, there are no JV partners mailing for it, it's not the kind of critical mass media, attention-getting endeavor that a product launch is.

And yet, you're still promoting, and many of the same kinds of email copy that you're going to write for a full-scale launch will exist in this campaign.

Then there is the campaign sequence that I like to refer to as the "meter-mover." You might want to increase the number of comments on your blog post, for instance, so you send emails that have a call to action asking people to comment on a blog post or on a podcast episode … or you may ask them to share something via social media, on Twitter, Facebook, Google Plus or LinkedIn. These are all email broadcasts that are designed to move the meter on one or more of these particular channels.

EMAIL TYPE 2: AUTOMATED CAMPAIGN SEQUENCES

What about campaign sequences that are *automated*? These are similar, but the difference is they're not taking place in real time. They're not being written "on the fly." You're not able to make timely references to current events, or respond to people's emails because all your messages are preloaded.

An *onboarding sequence* is a good example. An *onboarding sequence* is a series of emails that you write that introduces people into your way of thinking, into your worldview, and helps them get to know, like, and trust you. This may be a series of seven to upwards of 30 emails. The construction of such a sequence would be a book of its own.

Next is the *pre event autoresponder sequence,* which I call "the tractor beam" sequence. If you're a Star Trek fan you know a tractor beam is the magnetic space-beam the Starship Enterprise used to draw other objects and ships to herself. That's what a pre-event autoresponder sequence does – it draws prospects toward you.

The most visible example of this might be if you're holding a webinar to promote the launch of your product. Leading up to the webinar, you might have an email you send out to get people to sign up for the webinar, and then after they sign up, they're placed on your email list and they receive a 4-7 email *pre-event autoresponder sequence* that is sent out over a period of 4-7 days. This sequence sells them on the benefit of actually *attending* the webinar they just signed up for.

Next is the *post event autoresponder sequence* that I call 'the pattern buffer' sequence. The pattern buffer term also comes from the Star Trek TV series (might as well stick with the theme, right?). The Starship Enterprise used a technology called the *transporter,* which was a beam used to transport people from one place to another. When the person was taken into the transporter mechanism, they were "disassembled' at the atomic level and then reassembled at their destination (usually the planet below).

In the meantime, where *were* they? They were in what was called the "pattern buffer," the "memory" of the transporter device. My point is that the particular people on your list we're now discussing are those who signed up for your event, but for some reason didn't buy the thing you were selling.

What happens to them? Do we just abandon them to outer space? Let their molecules dissipate into the vastness of the universe? Or do we hold them in the "pattern buffer" with the hopes of being able to reassemble them as a customer at some point in the future? That's exactly what we do, we put them in the pattern buffer... and that's exactly what a *post event autoresponder sequence* is – a series of emails that happen *after* the event. This sequence either points them back to a replay of the webinar (in this example), or to another piece of content in another format which may be more appealing to them.

Why is this important? If they didn't attend your webinar, maybe it's because they hate webinars. Maybe they wanted the information so much that they signed up for the webinar and then realized how much they dislike webinars and decided not to attend.

What do you do? Maybe you make a video replay available to them. Maybe you make a PDF version of the information available as an eBook or white paper. Maybe you do a teleconference call. Maybe you have a short edited version where, if they don't want to watch a 60-90 minute webinar, maybe you have 10 minute video they can watch. The point is, you give them other options for consuming the material. This may give you a better chance of communicating the sales message to them. We see on average 20-30% of our sales come through the post event autoresponder sequence.

What about the people who bought? For them, there is the *post-sale autoresponder sequence*. You might ask why that's important. They already bought, why would you bother them? You might worry that this will remind them they bought it, and then maybe they'll ask for a refund. The whole point of the post-sale autoresponder sequence is actually to *solidify* the sale…

- To remind them of **why** they bought the product or service they purchased.
- To get them **to use the product or service** they purchased, because of the benefits.
- To **prevent** them from asking for a **refund**.

YOUR MARKETING A.R.M.

That's why I call these *post-sale autoresponder sequences* the "automated retention machine." You want to retain their business, so this automated retention machine (A.R.M.) reaches out to put your arm around them, and allows you to walk alongside them, saying, "You bought this for a reason, it's going to help you. Let me show you *how* to use it so you actually get the help you *wanted*."

This is an important sequence that you should write for each product you sell. Firstly, so you have a lower incidence of refunds and secondly, so that the people actually use what you sold them and benefit from it.

If that happens, then they will be more likely to buy something *else* from you in the future!

EMAIL TYPE 3: "ONE OFF" BROADCAST EMAILS

Next is the "social equity refill machine of niceness"… admittedly it's a long name, and I came up with the name so I could make the acronym "S.E.R.M.O.N." Why a sermon? You're preaching to them to get them to come back to "church."

SOCIAL EQUITY REFILL MACHINE OF NICENESS

What on earth am I talking about? The S.E.R.M.O.N. is a series of emails that are sent out with no intention to get them to sign up for any new list. No intention to get them to sign up for a webinar. No intention to get them to buy anything.

These are emails that *just spread good will,* that *give them something free.*

Maybe it's a free video training that you made for them just because you thought it would be helpful.

Maybe you send them an email to someone *else's* free training (and not as an affiliate). Maybe you saw an awesome TED talk that you thought they might find useful or inspiring. You can send that to them and it creates good will. It refills your "social equity account" with them… just because you were nice to them.

Thus: "social equity refill machine of niceness."

Now, I've told you about these sequences. You understand what they're for. They can have any number of emails in them. Any of these sequences can be three emails long, five, seven, fourteen or thirty. I know some of my clients that have email sequences that stretch out for a year and even two into the future, for each of these particular kinds of sequences.

So get to work on writing those sequences!

Next up – 21 "power tips" for crafting emails that sell.

21 KEYS TO POWERFUL EMAILS THAT SELL

These are principles for writing your emails, as well as mechanics of how to send campaigns, etc. If you follow them, you'll get much better results from your email marketing. These are the principles you need to follow when writing your marketing emails.

1. Use E-mail marketing to build permission-based lists

This might seem to be basic, might seem like email 101, but there are always new people coming on board to the online business world who don't understand that sending email of a commercial nature (which is: email that asks people to buy something, email that could be considered advertising, email sent without permission) is called *spam*.

Spam is not only impolite, it's actually against the law. Make sure you comply with the spam laws and only send emails to people who ask for them.

2. Use a reputable email delivery service

To send email to a large subscriber list, you simply can't use the Apple mail app on your Mac or the Outlook app on your Windows machine. You can't do it. You need to use a company that specializes in delivering email marketing, a company that automates the process of people subscribing to your email list and unsubscribing from receiving emails.

All of that needs to be automated. And not only that, companies like AWeber, InfusionSoft, Mail Chimp and more, all have compliance departments that ensure your email is compliant with the spam laws. They also make sure that your emails are getting delivered. They keep you off the spam blacklists.

So, for all these reasons, you definitely want to use a reputable email delivery service. There are many good ones. I've named three and there are many more. It doesn't matter too much which one you pick, as long as they're reputable, well known and have been around for a while. They're going to take care of all the hard stuff for you. Choose one and stick with it.

I say stick with it, because moving from email service provider to email service provider is difficult.

Which means, if you have thousands of people on your email list and you change from AWeber to InfusionSoft, you're inevitably going to lose people in the transfer. So it's better to pick a provider and stick with them from day one. I promise you whatever provider you pick you'll have complaints about them, you'll have problems with their service. Some part of what they do isn't going to suit you exactly right, but it's probably not worth switching providers over, unless it's critical to your business, because of the inconveniences and loss of email subscribers that I just explained.

3. Give web visitors reasons to opt- in, and set their expectations properly

People aren't going to give you their email address just to "get your newsletter," because they believe you're going to spam them.

You must offer them a compelling reason for them to want to opt in. A report, a video, a mini-course. Something.

If I sign up for your email newsletter and I have an expectation that you're going to deliver helpful information, and not advertisements, but you send me one promotion after another, I'll feel like it's spam. If I feel like its spam, then it *is* spam. Maybe not legally, but practically and emotionally it is. This means I won't like you and I will unsubscribe. Even worse, I'll stay on your list, eat up your bandwidth and I'll never read your emails.

So give web visitors reasons to opt-in and explain to them what they're going to be receiving. If they're signing up to get a premium, like a checklist or an eBook, video or whatever your email opt-in magnet might be, then make sure they understand that they're *also* signing up for your email newsletter, in which you will tell them about interesting news, tidbits and helpful pieces of information. Then, you will also tell them about special offers that you have available regarding your products and promotions.

Make it clear and up front.

4. Avoid Spam Complaints with Frequent, Consistent Mailings.

Surprising as it sounds, mailing more often can reduce spam complaints. That's because when you mail frequently and consistently, your readers won't forget who are are! If they sign up for your list and they don't hear from you for six weeks, and then you send them an email – bam! Spam complaint!

5. *Use* autoresponders *as robotic sales agents*

Again, you probably know what an autoresponder is, but in case you don't: this is a program that automatically sends a timed sequence of emails to anyone who subscribes.

It could be one email a day for seven days. It could be one email a day for 30 days. It could be one email every other day for 45 days. You determine the frequency and you can even make it on specific days after the initial sign-up. It's a preplanned, preprogrammed, preloaded sequence that's delivered automatically to each person in your email list, based on when they signed up for your email list.

This is very powerful, especially if you're using sequences to introduce people to you, your company and your services and let them get to know you through a series of storytelling or illustrative emails.

6. *Give people an unusually great reason to opt- in*

We talked earlier about *why* people opt-in. They opt-in for that opt-in or lead "magnet," something you're giving away that prompts them to want to give up their email address in order to get the thing you're giving away.

Work harder than other marketers to create Lead Magnets of Unusual Value. Go beyond what everyone else is offering. Offer a Lead Magnet that is as good as someone else's paid product. I think you should offer, not only the premium that you're giving away, but also "sell" your subscribers on the value of the email newsletter itself.

7. Give people great reasons to stay on your list

This is one that lots of people miss. I see this mark missed many times by people who don't understand that just because I signed up for their email list doesn't mean I'm going to stay signed up. Or maybe I will stay on board, but I won't read the emails delivered to my inbox. They may even show as being opened because I see them in my preview pane in my mail app, but I never really read them, and instead delete or archive them.

Don't take it for granted that anybody is interested in reading your next email. Give them a reason to *want* to read it. Make sure when you write the subject line for that email that you're writing it in such a way that makes people want to open the email. We'll talk more about that later.

8. Ask for a "sale" in every email

This doesn't necessarily mean you're asking them to pay money to buy a product, but you do want people to get into the habit of clicking on a link in every email you send. The point of this is that you may have them click on a link to watch a video, or to read a blog article, or see a funny cartoon. Most of the time these links may not be to your own material.

Maybe the links go to other resources, other websites, other people's materials on the web that's freely available, so you're not stealing anyone's material. You're linking to something they published publicly. Believe me, no author of any blog is going to get upset if you send traffic to their blog. No YouTube creator is going to get upset that you sent people to their video.

You want your readers to be in the habit of knowing that every time they get an email from you, there's always something interesting to click on. You send 10 messages that have a cool video, tip or article or something that benefits them and they click on the links time after time... and then when you send the next email, that has a link to one of your products or your product launch sequence, then they'll click on that link, too.

The instant assumption they make is that this too is something valuable that I want to watch, read or experience. It's important that you're asking for a sale in every email. Usually the sale will be a click on a link.

9. Craft a powerful signature file for all your emails

Most people won't read your signature file. Don't think this is going to revolutionize your business. It is real estate you can use, so why not use it? Why not, in your signature file, have a link to your website, your blog, podcast, other products, surveys or special deals? I think it's good sense to use that real estate effectively, even if only one person per month makes an extra purchase that they wouldn't have otherwise made. If you don't use your email signature file then you wouldn't get that one sale, which is maybe 12 additional sales per year. What would that be worth to you? Maybe it's even more than one. It's wasted if you don't use it.

10. Use broadcast emails for promotions

We've covered automated emails, using timed autoresponder sequences. Don't forget about the broadcast email, the email you send out "live" to your entire list. The value of sending a "live" email is you can reference current events, things that happened today in the news or on the calendar.

This provides proof this email was written today, that it's not automated. This makes your emails fresh and timely, and much more powerful than they would be otherwise.

11. *Know your Most Wanted Response*

What do I mean by the "Most Wanted Response" (or MWR)? Just this: if the reader only does one thing as a result of reading this email, what is that?

It needs to be *one* thing. What is the *one thing* that you most want them to do?

- Do I want them to click a link?
- Do I want them to hit reply and send me a message back?
- Do I want them to take a survey?
- Do I want them to make a purchase?

Know what your **most wanted response** is for every email that you send before you even craft it.

12. *Use only one MWR per email*

This is one of the most commonly made mistakes in email marketing. Most marketers send emails that have three or four different links to various offers and pages. That means their email has three or four different objectives. They're trying to accomplish several things with one email and it's confusing to the mind of the person receiving the email.

There's one principle we know about the psychology of selling for sure: the confused mind decides *nothing*. If you make too many requests of a reader in a single email, they will delete the email and move on to something else. They *won't* click on anything or make any decision.

So use only one **most wanted response** and only **one call to action** in your email. You maybe have more than one link to the call to action in that email, but only one action that you're asking for.

13. Craft subject lines using the P.A.C. formula

P.A.C. stands for Personal – Anticipation - Curiosity

You want each email to feel very personal to the recipient, and that doesn't *necessarily* mean you use the person's name. It means you speak to them in a way that's relevant to the material they were interested in when they signed up for your list. You're speaking their language, and talking about the subjects of deepest interest to your core audience.

Anticipated means that you've set up an expectation. You've written emails in the past that were so interesting, so intriguing that when they read your subject lines for each new email, they anticipate something interesting, something useful, or something profitable.

Curiosity is obvious, in that you write subject lines that arouse the curiosity of the reader. Your reader is asking...

"I wonder what that formula is that he mentions in the subject line?"

"I wonder what the new idea is that she wants to tell me about?"

"I wonder what it is that's so urgent that I have to read this email today?"

14. Start each email with an undeniable, confirmable truth

This is important and often overlooked. It's very powerful. One of the hurdles we have to overcome is skepticism and the fact that our readers often don't believe us... or aren't *sure* if they believe us.

One way to overcome that is to begin each email you send with a very firm, incontrovertible truth. It could be today's date. Most email delivery services provide you with a way to stamp the current date on the email on the day in which it's received.

That way when the recipient opens the email it has today's date as the first line. That is an incontrovertible truth. Or, you could start with something like... "Ray Edwards here writing to you." That's a truth that's incontrovertible, it *is* in fact coming from me, so you *know* it's true.

It could be, "I know what you're thinking as you're sitting there reading this email, you're wondering what it's about." You have to be careful with rhetorical statements like this because they may or may not be true, but saying you're "sitting in front of your computer right now," or "on your smartphone or tablet reading this email," is fairly safe. It's probably going to be true for 99% of people reading the email. (No, I'm not quite sure how the other 1% are reading your email.)

I know this sounds ridiculous, but I've tested it myself and proven to my satisfaction that starting with some fact, lends more legitimacy to your email. This makes the response you get to that email higher and more positive.

15. Use headline techniques, but not headline formatting for subject lines

It's okay to use headline templates to create subject lines, but don't format them like a headline or title. In a headline we use what's called "title case," all the words are capitalized except for the articles and conjunctions. Use regular *sentence* case in your subject lines, just like you do when you write a regular email to a friend. In fact, I often will use NO capitalization or punctuation at all in my subject lines, because that's the way friends write subject lines and emails. I want my email to look as though it comes from a friend.

16. Put the main benefit in the lead with a link

The lead for your email is anything that appears in the "preview pane" of most email clients. If the reader isn't using the preview pane then the rule of thumb is that the lead is the first sentence or two of your email. Put a link in the lead that accompanies the main benefit.

The point is, when someone opens the email, there's a link available right at the top, before they have to do any scrolling. That's not the only link you want in the email, and you don't want to be obnoxious about it, but you do want that link available to them right up top.

17. Use a PS that summarizes the lead benefit and provides a link

I know there's a lot of controversy in PS's in sales letters and in emails. Some people feel that it's cliché and overdone and doesn't make any sense, because why would you put a PS in an email when you can always go back and put whatever you want to in the actual *body* of the email.

The "PS" originated when people wrote letters on paper with ink and couldn't erase what they had written. If they wanted to add something, they used a "post-script" ("after written" or "P.S.").

What's the use for the PS in today's modern age? I don't know for sure, but I do know it works as a marketing tool. My *theory* is that with sales letters and emails alike, people often scroll to the bottom of the page or the bottom of the email to see what's for sale, and how much it costs. It certainly doesn't hurt to have a PS there for them, along with a clear call to action.

18. Place a minimum of 3 links to your call to action in the email body

This includes the link you put in the lead and the link in the PS. You want one additional link somewhere in the body of the email.

Don't overdo it. Don't use 15 links in an email. Three is a target. If you're sending a short email, you may only want to use one.

19. Use short emails that create the "Zeigarnik effect"

Zeigarnik is the last name of a psychologist who studied the quirk of human memory that deals with "open loops." We tend to remember more about subjects that are unresolved. The example used in the

Zeigarnik study was one of restaurant waiters and waitresses who still had a ticket open.

For a party they were serving with an unpaid check, the server tended to remember the details of the customer's order. What they had to eat, what stage of the meal they were in, etc. They remembered all those things and perhaps even remembered the name of the people at the table. However, once the check was closed and paid, and the guest had left, they could no longer remember the details of that particular party or order.

Why was that? It's the same reason that cliffhangers work in weekly TV series. You tune in because psychologically you "need" to close those loops.

How do you create this effect in email marketing? There are two simple ways you can do it.

First, you can tell a story in an email, and leave the next part of the story for the next email. You could just write, "that's all the time I have right now, if you want to find out what happened to Jack, you'll have to look for tomorrow's email where I explain the rest of the story."

That's the Zeigarnik effect, stretching them from one email to the next. Or, you could write, "I don't want to put the rest of this in email, but I've posted it on my website so click here to get the rest of the story."

That's the Zeigarnik effect that pulls readers straight to a web page. Perhaps even a sales video. You're using the desire that human beings have to close these open loops, and using it to get people to read the next email or to click the link.

20. Send emails that look like they were sent by a friend
Make the email look and feel as though it's coming from a friend. When friends send us an email, it doesn't usually come with a logo, stock images, and starbursts screaming SALE! or 25% OFF NOW THROUGH MONDAY!

21. Always honor unsubscribe requests

This should go without saying — and probably should have come earlier in the list. If people want to be unsubscribed from your list, don't get upset. You don't *want* them on the list, because they're just going to cause you problems, and they will think you're an annoying pest. Stop it!

This is part of all major email service providers; they actually force this auto-unsubscribe link to appear at the bottom of all your emails. That way whenever you send an email out it always has an unsubscribe link. Be aware that not everyone reads the words that say... "to unsubscribe click here."

Occasionally someone will send you an angry email asking you to take them off the list and to stop "spamming" them. Your temptation will be to email them back and say, "What, can't you *read*? Didn't you see the line at the bottom of the email that said 'click here to unsubscribe'? Just click the link."

Don't send emails like that because it's not worth your time, and it's insulting. Just click the link for them, unsubscribe *for* them and say no more. Problem solved.

Those are the 21 principles of powerful emails that sell. **And now, one more principle, which will help you** preserve your peaceful state of calm, relaxed creativity.

FINALLY, THE ZEN MASTER'S EMAIL RULE: DON'T READ COMPLAINT E-MAILS

This doesn't mean that I'm suggesting that you ignore legitimate complaints from your readers, subscribers and customers. Those should be taken care of right away, but not by you. If you're the marketer, the copywriter, the one creating... the last thing you need are people sending evil, nasty messages that are deriding your character, criticizing your work and making you feel bad. You don't need to read emails that are a big fat bummer. It's not good for your psychology or your business.

Those emails *need* to be read, but *not by you.*

My assistant has a standing rule from me, "I will read any email that requires my attention, any email that is positive feedback, or that will make me feel good about my work. I do **not** want to read any emails that are negative in nature. Please do whatever needs to be done to make that person happy."

My assistant also knows if there's a *real* reason I need to be involved, *even if it's negative*, I want to hear about it. So she filters out 95% of all the negative criticism emails I get, because it doesn't help me, or help the other person for me to hear those emails.

If it's a criticism or complaint she feels I need to hear about, she will often summarize it in kinder, gentler language and pass it along to me.

The point: don't ignore people. Take care of your customers, satisfied or unsatisfied. Be careful of your own mental hygiene and psychology. There's no need to read your critics' remarks if they're just going to bring you down and cause the quality of your work to deteriorate.

CHAPTER 4 QUICK SUMMARY:

21 Keys to Persuasive Autoresponders and E-mails

1. **Use E-mail Marketing to Build Permission-Based Lists.** Prospects who give you permission to market to them are most likely to buy. Honor (and widen) the circle of permission.

2. **Use a Reputable E-mail Delivery Service.** If your e-mail doesn't get delivered, you won't make any sales; getting it delivered is a full-time job.

3. **Give Web Visitors Reasons To Opt- In, And Set Their Expectations Properly.** You must offer some sort of premium to entice visitors to give up their names and e-mail addresses.

4. **Avoid Spam Complaints with Frequent, Consistent Mailings.** Surprising as it sounds, mailing more often can reduce spam complaints.

5. **Use Autoresponders as Robotic Sales Agents.** A sequence of contacts is a powerful way of delivering your sales message.

6. **Give People an Unusually Great Reason To Opt- In.** Work harder than other marketers to create Lead Magnets of Unusual Value.

7. **Give People Great Reasons to Stay On Your List.** Don't take it for granted that anybody is interested in reading your next email. Give them a reason to want to read it.

8. **Ask for a "Sale" in Every E-mail.** Treat each e-mail like a miniature sales letter; just be clear what the call to action is for that particular e-mail. Get them in the habit of clicking on your links!

9. **Craft a Powerful Signature File for All E-mails.** This is a powerful action device. Don't forget it.

10. **Use Broadcast E-mails for Promotions.** Broadcasts are great for promotions and launch sequences (time-bound offers).

11. **Know Your Most Wanted Response.** If you don't know it, how can you elicit the desired behavior?

12. **Use Only One MWR Per Email.** The confused mind never buys.

13. **Craft Subject Lines Using the PAC Formula.** Write your subject lines so that they are personal, fulfill anticipation, and arouse curiosity.

14. **Start Each E-mail with Undeniable, Confirmable Truth.** For instance, you might start with the date; subtle credibility.

15. **Use Headline Techniques, but Not Headline Formatting.** Avoid making your e-mail look like an ad.

16. **Put the Main Benefit in the Lead, with a Link.** The first paragraph is the lead, and you should have a link to your MWR in that paragraph (or following it).

17. **Use a PS That Summarizes the Main Benefit and Provides a Link.** Just like in your sales letter, the PS may be the only copy in your e-mail the prospect reads.

18. **Place a Minimum of 3 Links to Your Call to Action in the E-mail Body.** The first two will get most of the clicks.

19. **Send Short E-mails That Create Zeigarnik Effect.** Your MWR is most likely to get the prospect to visit a Web page.

20. **Send Emails That Look Like They Were Sent by a Friend.** You want your emails to look like those of a friend, not like sales fliers or newspaper ads.

21. **Always Honor Unsubscribe Requests.** Avoid needless headaches.

The Zen Master's Email Rule:

Don't Read Complaint E-mails. And whatever you do, don't get involved in replying; have someone on your staff do it for you. Preserve your peaceful state of calm, relaxed creativity.

---

*Claim **your FREE membership** (retail value $197) including a growing library of templates & tutorials, visit CopyThatSellsBook.com (no credit card required).*

5

HOW TO WRITE BULLET POINTS THAT VIRTUALLY FORCE YOUR PROSPECTS TO BUY

"It's simple. You just take something and do something to it, and then do something else to it. Keep doing this and pretty soon you've got something."

—Jasper Johns

B ullet points are crucial to the success of your online sales copy. They are one of the most under-used, yet most powerful, persuasion weapons in your copywriting arsenal. It seems almost no one understands their full value.

Just today, I had a telephone review with a potential client. We were looking through the sales copy for his product. I immediately identified one of the major problems with that particular copy: no bullet points.

Bullet points make your copy easier to read. They make your benefits easier for your readers to digest and personalize. Therein lies the magic of copywriting—getting your readers to imagine themselves enjoying the benefits. That's 90 percent of the work.

I really like the quote at the beginning of this chapter, because in many ways, when we're writing copy, it feels like that's what we're doing. We're taking something—this idea, this copy we're working on—and we just do *something* to it, and then do something *else* to it, and pretty soon we've actually *got* something.

One of the first "somethings" you can do, especially if you are at a loss as to where to start writing, is to just write … *something*! I've gone on record as saying I don't believe in writer's block. It's true; I don't believe in it, and I don't suffer from it.

It's because when I'm stuck, I pick things I *can* write. If I sit down in front of my computer (or with a legal pad, which is sometimes how I write), and I can't think of anything to write and I start feeling that resistance to writing, I just write things I *know* I can write.

It might be as simple as writing out the guarantee. It might be writing out the website URL, the mailing address, or phone number—*anything* that gets your pen moving or your keyboard clicking. Bullet points are a *great* place to start writing when you're in that "stuck place," when that resistance-to-writing feeling sneaks up on you.

Let me give you three things you can do right away to get you started creating great bullet points, even if you feel as though you don't have anything to write at this particular moment.

1) Start a bullet swipe file

I encourage you to start swipe files whenever you find good copy that you respond to. Start saving the e-mails you receive that catch your interest and make you want to read them. Notice the commonalities of those e-mails that make that happen.

Start saving your snail mail. I'm not talking about the coupons you get from the pizza parlor down the street. I'm talking about promotions you get for magazine and newsletter subscriptions, information on products, bigger ticket items that really catch your attention and make you want to open the envelope.

WHAT IS A "SWIPE FILE"?

According to Wikipedia, "A **swipe file** is a collection of tested and proven advertising and sales letters. Keeping a **swipe file** (templates) is a common practice used by advertising copywriters and creative directors as a ready reference of ideas for projects."

Source: https://en.wikipedia.org/wiki/**Swipe_file**

The key point to keep in mind is that s swipe file is a "ready reference of ideas," not a file to use for plagiarism! Study and emulate the styles, techniques, and underlying structures – but never just copy another writer's words. That's stealing, and aside from being wrong, it's also illegal. Swipe responsibly!

One final thought on swipe files that should be obvious, but deserves to be mentioned: keep your own successful copy from past work in your swipe file!

This is good direct-response copy, so every facet of copy deserves its own swipe file. Bullet points are no different. You'll want to start building a swipe file of great headlines, of great sales letters, and of great e-mails. Likewise, I urge you to start a swipe file that focuses specifically on copy that features great bullet points, because it's some of the most important copy you will write.

2) Write at least 105 bullets of your own

Now, I'm going to make this easy for you, because in this chapter, I'm going to give you twenty-one templates to help you write bullets. All you have to do is write five of each type from the checklist, and you'll have your 105 bullets.

3) Select your best bullets

Pick thirty-five—the top one-third—of those bullets. Choose the ones that really "sing," the ones that have that kind of poetry that you feel makes a good bullet. After this chapter, you should know what makes a good bullet, so you'll be able to make that judgment intelligently.

Let's talk about the function of bullet points. What *are* bullet points? What do they do for your copy, and why is it important for you to include them? You've seen bullet points in copy, I'm sure. Especially if you've ever read any of my material. I use a lot of bullet points in my copy.

A bullet point is simply a one or two-line sentence that's defined by a bullet, a round circle, a checkmark, or perhaps a little box next to it, that sets it apart from the rest of the text. The reason for using bullets in our copy is very simple.

Earlier, we discussed the fact that there are three things people never do when first reading your copy. They never *read* anything at first; they never *believe* anything at first; and they never *do* or *buy* anything at first.

We know they don't read your copy. They skim the copy. They scan through it. They scroll through it. To get them to start reading, we use devices to capture their attention. One of those devices is the headline. That's what gets their attention initially to get them to read the rest of the ad, copy, or sales page.

The next devices are the subheads, the smaller headlines throughout the copy that telegraph the message of your sales copy.

The third device we use to get people to stop skimming, scanning, and scrolling—and start reading—are *bullet points*.

When they're scanning copy, especially online, readers' eyes are drawn to text surrounded by white space or that text looks different from the surrounding copy – for instance, text set apart by bullet points. Write your bullet points carefully so they're not too wordy, just one or two lines in most cases, so they are quickly digestible.

People can take that in, almost at a glance, and that's where you have the opportunity to start the process of getting your readers to imagine or picture themselves enjoying the benefits that your product or service offers them.

This is the reason we use bullet points in our copy. If you look at successful promotions, off-line or online, almost without fail you'll find that the most successful pieces of copy use lots of bullet points. That is not an accident.

As copywriters, we take note of the clues that are left behind by successful marketing campaigns. Here's a clue: successful promotions use lots of bullet points, and so should we.

For any one piece of sales copy, you should use a minimum of three to five different *kinds* of bullet points. This is another of the more common rookie mistakes I see—having the same *kinds* of bullet points stacked up on top of one another.

That becomes monotonous and defeats the purpose of having bullet points in your copy to begin with. If we use the same language to spell out each bullet point, they all start to sound alike. The redundancy reduces the impact. Mix up the *kinds* of bullet points; break up the monotony with a variety of different approaches.

Always write at least three times as many bullets as you think you will need. That way, you can choose only the best ones for your final copy. Many top copywriters will write many more times that number of bullets. In fact, I was having dinner with copywriting pro Parris Lampropoulos recently and he told me the first thing he does for any copy package he's working on is write 500-700 bullets! Then he circulates that list to a half dozen people and asks them to pick their favorite 25-50. Paris told me some people end up choosing 75-100 "favorites," and it's easy for him to then select the top 75-150 bullet points to use in his first draft.

Think about that. A lot of work? Yes, but does it yield the very best, most response-getting bullets? You bet it does.

So, how many different types of bullet points *are* there? Well, there are probably hundreds, but my list for you here consists of twenty-one. This list should be comprehensive enough to serve the needs of most entrepreneurial copywriters. At least it will get you started, and give you time to start building your own swipe file and templates.

There's a "master bullet type" that most of these bullets will fall under, called the "blind" bullet. What is a blind bullet? A blind bullet is a bullet that tantalizes your reader with a curiosity-inducing statement, yet does not reveal the actual secret behind it, in effect setting up an "open loop" that the mind longs to complete. A void of curiosity that leaves the reader thinking, "I want to know the answer behind that particular bullet." That is one of the things that make bullets so incredibly effective. The only way to know the answer for sure is to buy the product!

There are bullets that are *not* blind, and I'll refer to those as "naked" bullets. It's not anything saucy; it's simply that we're *revealing* information in naked bullets, whereas blind bullets are *concealing* information but hinting in specific ways about that information.

21 WINNING BULLET POINT TEMPLATES

1) The "Wrong" Bullet.

What do I mean by the "wrong" bullet? The wrong bullet is simply a case where you can contradict a common assumption. You get the reader to state a belief that he or she has, then you tell them, "Wrong!"

For instance, if you're writing copy for health products, perhaps a nutritional supplement that is designed to reduce high blood pressure, then you might write a bullet that says something like this:

- *Eating lots of salt in your diet is bad for your blood pressure, right?* **Wrong!** *We'll explain why when you order our special report.*

You can see why contradicting a commonly held assumption captures the attention of the reader and makes him or her want to know the secret behind the bullet. Of course you need to have some factual basis to back up the claim you're making. You can't make a claim that's controversial simply for the sake of controversy, unless you can back the claim up. Assuming that you can, this is a very effective bullet type to use.

2) The "Themed Sequence" bullet.

This is a case where you are going to spell out, for instance, the "seven deadly diet sins," or the "three humiliating secrets men don't want women to know."

How might you employ themed sequence bullets in your copy? You might have a section that reads like this:

The 7 Deadly Diet Sins That Keep You Fat
1. The three **foods you should** *never* **eat** that are recommended by almost every diet doctor. *Eat these foods, and you're* **sure** *to stay fat.*
2. Why the **time of day** you exercise is very important, and why most diet gurus have this information wrong.
3. *And so on…*

One quick note: just because they are *bullet* points doesn't mean you have to use actual bullets. Numbers work well, too. If you're spelling out the "three humiliating secrets men don't want women to know," then those bullets should be "1-2-3," instead of black circular dots or checkmarks.

3) The Two-step Bullet.

A two-step bullet offers a parenthetical elaboration on the main benefit statement. Let me explain. This parenthetical statement is the real magnet in the bullet.

When you have a blind bullet in your copy and you want to heighten the amount of curiosity that is aroused by it, after your initial bullet statement, in parentheses, make another statement that *really* makes people think about what it is you're trying to tell them.

For instance, if you're writing a sales letter about a product on networking, one of your bullets might say...

> **What to *never* do with your business card, and why.** (If you get this wrong, people will walk away and you'll never hear from them again.)

That's a parenthetical statement that heightens the curiosity and enhances or elaborates on the main benefit statement. The implied benefit behind this, of course, is, if you know these myths, you'll be able to avoid these mistakes, and therefore, people will remember you and will call you back.

This is an important point to remember: even when you are talking about mistakes people make, you're talking about benefits—because it's beneficial to learn to avoid them.

4) The Giveaway Bullet.

This one I don't see used very often, especially by new, inexperienced copywriters or marketers, because they don't want to give away their information.

Every now and then in your bullets you should give something away. Give them good information. In fact, I would go so far as to say, give away your *best* information. Give away your *best* tricks.

Don't be afraid to give away information, especially information that's self-explanatory in its value. Most marketers are afraid readers will know they've just received the best you have to offer and won't buy anything from you.

Research shows this is not the case. If you can give people a tip or trick that's stunningly good, they are more likely to think, "If that's what they're *giving away* in their sales promotion, what are they hiding behind the scenes? If the *free* stuff is this good, what kind of information do I get when I *pay* it?" You don't want to give away *all* of your best information, but giveaway bullets, used sparingly, are very effective at credentializing the value of your information.

5) *The Reverse Hook Bullet.*

This is a bullet that presents, first, an interesting fact, and then presents an unexpected benefit that arises from that interesting fact.

For instance, let's say you're in the pay-per-click marketing space and you're selling a pay-per-click marketing course that teaches people how to use Google AdWords to drive traffic to their site. One of the challenges in that marketplace is being able to select profitable keywords that generate enough traffic to yield measurable results.

So, you might be able to use a "reverse hook" bullet that's based on real statistical information. It might say something like, "37.1% of the keywords in your Google AdWords account are not getting enough traffic to give you reliable test data." Now, this is the parenthetical statement, "Here's a simple trick you can use to eliminate these keywords from your ad campaigns forever and save yourself loads of money."

That is a reverse hook bullet. It's an interesting fact that brings an unexpected benefit if you know how to use the information correctly.

6) *The Naked Benefit Bullet.*

This bullet makes a direct benefit claim, but it has got to be supported by some additional facts, or what I call "intrigues" that deepen your reader's interest. You may not be able to come up with a creative way to describe every single benefit you're writing bullets for in your sales copy.

You may just need to go ahead and talk directly about the benefit.

For instance, if you are selling a product on how to generate lots of creative ideas, your bullet point—which spells out a naked benefit— might be "how to effortlessly generate dramatically different ideas and know instantly if they are worth pursuing."

The benefit is being able to come up with good ideas.

7) *The Transactional Bullet.*

This is very similar to a headline template. It's simply a proposition that says, "Give me (X), and I'll give you (Y)." It might be something as simple as, "Give me one hour, and I'll teach you how to write effective headlines," or, "Give me three days, and I'll teach you how to buy property with no money down."

It's a *transaction*. Whenever you're using a transactional bullet, it's often best if you can use it in a case where what you're asking from your readers seems of small consequence in contrast to the benefit you're offering to them.

Let's say, for instance, you are writing copy for a product that offers training in how to use QuickBooks software, and this software teaches users of QuickBooks a simple way to automatically categorize their transactions. In fact, by using your method, they can do in five minutes what used to take them an hour each day to do.

Then you can say something like, "Give me 15 minutes, and I'll teach you how to save 45–55 minutes every day from now on." That's a transactional bullet that makes the transaction seem like a no-brainer for your prospect.

8) *The If-Then Bullet.*

In this bullet type, you're giving the prospect something *easy* for him or her to do or comply with, and you're associating it to a *more valuable* benefit.

For example:

- If you can spare 10 minutes a day, you can lose five pounds a month.

Or...

- If you can send or receive e-mail, then you can learn to make stock trades online in total safety.

You can also use this type of bullet as a qualifier:

- If you are over the age of 50 and have found it difficult to get life insurance, these three simple questions will often get you approved for a life insurance application.

Even though we're just going through twenty-one bullet types, I hope you can see that you can take each of these bullet types and mix them up and combine them in different ways. You really have hundreds of possible types of bullets you can use, so you're never again stuck for creativity.

You can always come back to this list and ask yourself, "What 'wrong' bullets can I write? What themed sequence bullets could I write? What two-step bullets could I write? What giveaway? What reverse hook? How can I write a naked benefit bullet?"

Some of them may duplicate one another and cross over, but that's okay, because you're expressing the same ideas in different ways. Then you can whittle these down to fine-tune your copy.

So remember when you're going through your bullet writing exercise, don't edit while you're writing—just write. If you sat down and wrote five bullets for each type, then you would have 105 bullets to choose from for your copy.

9) The "Truth About" Bullet.

This works especially well with any controversial question or issue that is hotly debated. Find an issue where the controversy is well-known in your market. For instance, in the weight loss market you could write about carbohydrates. As one of your bullet points in your weight loss product copy, you can say, "The truth about carbohydrates - and chances are, it's not what you think it is."

That's a great example of a polarized topic: the role carbohydrates play and how you should manage them in your diet. You can polarize people and catch their interest, whichever side of the issue they may fall upon, simply by using the "truth about" bullet.

10) The "Single Most" Bullet.

Use this type of bullet when you have a superior benefit that you can *prove*. Exercise a little bit of caution with this, because you want to make sure you truly do have the superior benefit and that you really can prove it.

If you have the fastest, easiest, and lowest risk way of lowering your blood pressure, then you should boldly say so: "The single fastest, easiest, and best way of lowering your blood pressure documented and approved by the American Medical Association."

Of course I don't know what that is; I'm making that copy up. *(I wish I knew what it was; I could make a fortune!)*

Just make *sure* you actually have the "single most" whatever-it-is you're touting. This is an effective way to talk about it. I guarantee if your product is the superior product in its category, you'll have the opportunity to use at least three or four "single most" bullets within your overall copy.

Give some very careful thought to this. It is a very powerful bullet technique if you don't overuse it.

11) *The "How-To" Bullet.*

This is a simple and very direct approach to writing a bullet. It's the most common type of bullet, and there's a reason why. It's easy to write, and it's effective, as long as you're a little more creative than the next copywriter is.

Here's what I mean. If you are writing copy for a product that is all about how to grow bigger, better, and more beautiful roses in your garden, you don't want to write a bullet that says, "How to grow better roses." You want a bullet that uses specificity to *dimensionalize* the benefit you're claiming.

What do I mean by "dimensionalize"? Make it three dimensional. *Make it real.* Saying "Grow more and better roses" isn't a dimensional statement. However, saying "How to grow rose bushes that are literally bursting with mounds of fragrant, colorful, beautiful blooms, with less effort and in less time" *dimensionalizes* that particular benefit bullet.

Any time you use the how-to bullet, make sure you're using a few more specifics and make it more real, more tangible to the reader.

12) *The Number Bullet.*

Use this when you have a specific number of techniques or multiple ways of doing a certain thing, multiple reasons why, or multiple reasons why *not*. Again, this is where you can combine a bullet with other kinds of bullets. You can combine the number bullet with the how-to bullet by simply saying, "Three ways to reduce your heating bill without making you or your family uncomfortable with the temperature of your house."

You're combining a number bullet with a how-to bullet. That's a great way to dimensionalize the how-to bullet. Another way to combine the number bullet with a different type of bullet is to go one step back and look at the "single most" bullet. You could simply say, "The three ways to get 10% better gas mileage from any vehicle with a simple adjustment you can make with a screwdriver."

13) *The Sneaky Bullet.*

You've seen this one. You want to use it when you can imply some kind of element of conspiracy. Be careful you don't overuse it, though.

So, what does the sneaky bullet look? Well, it would be something as easy and simple as "The sneaky methods drug companies use to keep you hooked on their products," "Three sneaky tricks used by furnace repairmen to drive up the cost of your maintenance," or "The one sneaky trick almost every auto mechanic uses to inflate your bill and how to avoid being suckered."

This is most effective when you can confirm a suspicion that your reader already has. If you can do so, he or she will immediately be inclined to side with you, because we all love it when other people throw rocks at our enemies and confirm our suspicions. We like being proven right.

14) *The "Better Than" Bullet.*

This is a great way to get your reader's attention. You want to find something good that you can make better. For instance, if you discovered a way to lose weight that was better than the Atkins Diet, you could say, "Better than Atkins."

Be ready to back that up, however. Especially in the health care field, you really have to be careful about complying with federal regulations when making any claims at all.

Consider this a word of caution about using this particular bullet with nutraceuticals, pharmaceuticals, exercise, and any other health-related products. Make sure you're following the rules of compliance with the FTC, the FDA, and any of the other "alphabet agencies."

Let's use a different example. You have a method of doing follow-up marketing that is superior to using e-mail autoresponders. This method of yours nets 100 percent deliverability of your follow-up messages.

Now, each of us knows that e-mail is far from being 100 percent delivered. There are estimates ranging anywhere from 15 to over 50 percent of e-mails not delivered to their intended recipient. This isn't spam we're talking about; this is e-mail that people *want* to receive.

If you could guarantee 100 percent deliverability, you would be able to boldly claim, "Better than e-mail!" Often an effective way to use the "better than" bullet is to simply use a colon. So you might say something like, "Better than e-mail: 100% delivery of your follow-up messages guaranteed!"

15) *The Simple Fact Bullet.*

When you can't use a blind bullet, use simple facts—but make them interesting. You want to present worst case scenarios to set these particular kinds of bullets up.

For instance, in the health care field there was a study that came out not too long ago that showed people with healthy arteries are susceptible to sudden death because of plaque within their arteries, even though they may not have hardening of the arteries, or arteriosclerosis.

Even without a blockage, inflammation within their arteries might cause little pieces of plaque to break off and suddenly block the artery and kill them.

A simple fact bullet, using that information, might say something like, "Healthy people are dying of sudden cardiac arrest," quote the study, then follow up with a comma and say something to this effect: "There are steps you can take to prevent this from happening."

That's a simple fact bullet. It's not much of a blind bullet, but by presenting that simple fact, you can help reinforce the value, and the curiosity factor.

16) The "What" Bullet.

I love these bullets because they're the easiest to use. It's a variation of the how-to bullet. The "what" bullet simply answers the question "What?" "What inoculations you need to travel abroad." "What you should avoid touching when you check into a hotel room." "What to do when you're audited by the IRS."

Can you see how easy it is to construct "what" bullets? These bullets are the easiest for you to write.

17) The "What NEVER" Bullet.

This is the negative form of the "what" bullet. Notice how it frequently plays on the fear factor.

- What never to eat on an airplane (unless you want to die).
- What never to do immediately after exercising (if you want to avoid having a heart attack).
- What never to do on a first date (if you want him to ever call you back).

You simply start by stating what one should never do, and then you follow that up with the possible consequences of the reader ignoring this brilliant "what never" advice.

18) The "Do You?" Bullet.

Use this particular kind of bullet when you believe your readers are doing something that is a mistake. Something that your product, service, or information will help them avoid.

"Do you make these mistakes when filling out your business tax returns?" Then you can use this as a two-step bullet by putting a parenthetical statement after that which says, "If you do, get ready to be audited — and you'd better have your records in order!"

19) The "Reason Why" Bullet.

It's a simple version of "reason why" copy. "Reason why" copy is a concept that is not often used, but should be. It's just explaining the reasons why they should buy your product or service. Why is your offer superior to another company's offer? Why should they buy now? Why should they buy from you?

"Reason why" is powerful advertising copy, and the "reason why" bullet is copy that *hides* the reason why.

A good example of "reason why" bullet point copy would be:

- The reason why you should always use the lowest octane fuel available at the gas pump, not the highest.

That arouses my curiosity. What is the reason *behind* that?

20) The "Secrets Of" Bullet.

If you have an unusual solution, device, tactic, or method, then you can use this bullet to build curiosity. This is another bullet you need to use with care. Overuse can erode your credibility.

If you do know secrets, then using this kind of bullet sparingly helps fuel the fire of curiosity and can be a powerful addition to the bullets that you're using in your copy.

21) The Probing Question Bullet.

Ask a question you are reasonably certain you know the answer to. This is somewhat similar to number eighteen, but eighteen is targeting the readers directly on something that you're pretty sure you know about them personally—either that they're making a certain mistake; that they're engaging in a certain behavior; or they have a certain problem.

This bullet isn't necessarily directed at a mistake they're making or behavior they're engaging in. It can simply be a question about whether, for instance, they have a specific kind of knowledge.

- Do you know the seven kinds of deductions the IRS looks for to flag your return for an audit?
- Do you know the three tricks to use at closing to save tens of thousands of dollars on your real estate transactions?
- Do you know the 21 kinds of bullets you can use in your copy that will make it stand superior to other copy and close more sales?

These are all probing question bullet points.

Now, how do you use this list of 21 Winning Bullet Point Templates when you're writing copy? Try what I suggested earlier: sit down and write five or ten of each of these bullets for your product.

If you get stuck and you only get three of them, that's okay—just move on. I would use a spiral-bound notebook or a legal pad and just move on to a different page. At the top of the page, write what kind of bullets you're writing. Again, if you get stuck, don't worry about it—just keep moving.

If you go through all twenty-one with this exercise, you're going to have twenty-one pages: some with ten bullets, some with two, some with five or seven, but you'll end up with many more than 100 bullets, and you can go back through and look at what you've written.

Pick out the ones that you think are outstanding and start migrating those to a different list. You will find you have a variety of bullets to choose from. I would suggest then you simply mix them up and group them on the page. I think it's most effective to break up your bullets into segments of ten or fifteen in a section on your page.

Instead of having fifty bullets in a row, I would break that up into five different lists of ten bullets each, using different bullet types in each of those sections of your copy, breaking that up with different subsections of your copy and paragraphs so the flow stays even. You don't want the flow of your copy to appear jagged.

By not appearing "jagged," I mean you don't want a section that has five big paragraphs followed by a section that is twenty bullets, followed by a section that's one paragraph, followed by a section that's another fifty bullets. You want a more even flow.

For example: two short paragraphs followed by a list of ten bullets, followed by another two short paragraphs, followed by a list of ten bullets. You want the rhythm of your copy to feel consistent.

CHAPTER 5 QUICK SUMMARY:

21 Bullet Point Templates You Can Use Today

1. **The "Wrong!" Bullet.** When you can contradict a common assumption, use the "wrong!" bullet.

2. **The "Themed Sequence" Bullet.** For instance, "7 Deadly Diet Sins" or "3 Humiliating Secrets Men Don't Want Women to Know."

3. **The "Two-Step" Bullet.** A two-step bullet offers a parenthetical elaboration on the main benefit statement. This parenthetical statement is the real "magnet" in the bullet.

4. **The "Giveaway" Bullet.** Every now and then, "give" them something.

5. **The "Reverse Hook" Bullet.** Interesting fact plus unexpected benefit.

6. **The "Naked Benefit" Bullet.** This bullet makes a direct benefit claim, but it must be supported by some additional facts or intrigues that deepen your reader's interest.

7. **The "Transactional" Bullet.** Simple transaction: "Give me … and I'll give you…"

8. **The "If… Then…" Bullet.** Give the prospect something easy for him or her to do or comply with—and associate it to a benefit.

9. **The "Truth About" Bullet.** Works with any controversial question, point, or issue.

10. **The "Single Most" Bullet.** When you have a provable superior benefit, use this kind of bullet.

11. **The "How-To" Bullet.** Simple and direct approach. This is the most common type of bullet.

12. **The "Number" Bullet.** Use this when you have a specific number of techniques, multiple ways of doing a certain thing, or multiple "reasons why."

13. **The "Sneaky" Bullet.** Use when you can imply an element of conspiracy.

14. **The "Better Than" Bullet.** A great way to get their attention; find something good that you can better.

15. **The "Simple Fact" Bullet.** When you can't use a "blind" bullet, use simple facts but make them interesting. Present "worst case" scenarios to set them up.

16. **The "What" Bullet.** A variation of the "how-to" bullet.

17. **The "What Never" Bullet.** The negative form of the "what" bullet; plays on the "fear factor."

18. **The "Do You?" Bullet.** Use when you think you know they are doing something that is a mistake (which your product avoids).

19. **The "Why" Bullet.** A simple version of "reason why" copy— that keeps the "reason why" hidden.

20. **The "Secrets Of" Bullet.** If you have an unusual solution, device, or tactic, use this bullet to build curiosity.

21. **The "Probing Question" Bullet.** Ask a question you are reasonably certain you know the answer to.

---

*Claim **your FREE membership** (retail value $197) including a growing library of templates & tutorials, visit CopyThatSellsBook.com (no credit card required).*

6

THE TRIAD THAT SELLS MORE: IRRESISTIBLE OFFERS, RISK REVERSAL, AND POWERFUL CLOSES

"People get caught up in wonderful, eye-catching pitches, but they don't do enough to close the deal. It's no good if you don't make the sale. Even if your foot is in the door or you bring someone into a conference room, you don't win the deal unless you actually get them to sign on the dotted line."

—Donald Trump

While it's true that proof elements, bullet points, and other factors enhance conversions on your website, you could construct a sales letter using nothing more than the following four elements:

- Headline
- Benefit-rich offer
- Convincing risk reversal proposal
- Pressure-cooker close

That's why you must pay attention to what I call *the triad of selling*—the offer, the close, and the risk reversal segment. These three elements support the entire structure of your ad. Remember, whatever copy we're writing is an ad whether it's a sales letter, e-mail, landing page, or even an eBay ad—they're *all* ads.

We'll dive deeper into writing closing copy and guarantees in the next two chapters, but for now...

Here are twenty-one steps to writing irresistible offers, rock-solid *risk reversal* copy, and powerful closes:

1) Make your offer stand alone.

Think of it this way. If the offer section is the only part of your sales letter that your prospects read, can they make a buying decision? You should be giving them all the information they need to make a buying decision.

Construct your offer so it's like a miniature sales letter. It needs a headline, a little deck copy, a string of benefit-rich bullets that describe what the product is about, and exactly what your prospects are going to get when they buy.

Then give them a call to action, where they can click and actually order your product or service.

2) Apply the P.A.S.T.O.R. Framework™ to your offer.

Here's a brief recap of the P.A.S.T.O.R. Framework from chapter 1:

1. **Person, Problem, Pain**: Identify the person you are writing to, the problem that your product or service is intended to solve, and the pain your person is experiencing.
2. **Amplify**: Stress the consequences of what will happen if that problem isn't solved.

3. **Story and Solution**: Tell the story of someone who has solved that problem, using your solution.

4. **Transformation and Testimony**: Articulate the results that your product or service will bring, providing real-life testimonials to strengthen your case.

5. **Offer**: Describe exactly what you are offering for sale, focusing on the transformation instead of on the deliverables (the "stuff").

6. **Response**: Ask the customer to buy, with step-by-step instructions telling them what to do next.

3) Enclose your order area copy in a differentiating text box.

In old-style direct mail, this looks like a coupon you might clip out from a newspaper or magazine. There's often a dashed border around the edge of this "order area." In the old newspaper or magazine ad, this indicated the part of the page to cut out with a scissors and mail in with your payment. But I'm willing to bet you've seen these dashed-border style "offer boxes" on web sales pages. Why does this work online? Why is it that so many websites use this device? Nobody needs the "clipping guide" on a web page. The answer is … I don't really know!

I suspect it's a visual cue that we've linked up in our nervous system that says, "Oh, this is where they're going to talk about what it is I'm supposed to get if I buy their product or service." I think we've probably been trained over the years to think that this is what an offer is supposed to look like.

But, the truth is it doesn't *matter* why. It simply matters that it is effective. It's another case of not worrying too much about whether we think it's aesthetically pleasing, whether we like the way it looks or not, but realizing that it *does* work and that effectiveness is what we're after with our sales copy.

4) Use the prospect's positive voice in the offer.

Give your prospects the words to say inside their own minds.

I'd like you to take a moment and imagine you're looking at a page on a website or in a book. You're reading the words on that page. You look at the page; the light reflects off the page and into your eyes; that signal is sent to your brain; your brain looks at the symbols on the page and interprets them as words; and your inner voice speaks the words in your mind.

Think about the power of that. This is why copy works. You are thinking thoughts *for* the reader. If you don't believe that, I'd like you to go back and reread what I wrote in the paragraph above. Isn't it true that you're thinking the thoughts I *told* you to think?

The reason this is so powerful when related to offers is that when you write in the prospect's positive voice ("Yes, Ray, I want to take advantage of your Copywriting Academy Coaching Program. I want to possess the power of turning words into wealth."), you're *telling* him or her what to think. Even more, I would submit you're *thinking* the thoughts *for* him or her, using your voice.

The mind is the instrument that your voice is played on.

5) Use aspirational language.

Invoke your reader's desire. Focus on the outcome your reader desires and use language that aspires to that outcome, to gain the emotional state or the sense of being that this outcome will give them.

For instance, an aspiration is contained within the words I just gave you from the offer for Copywriting Academy Coaching Program, the copy that says, "Yes, I want to possess the power of turning words into wealth."

6) Use credit card logos and secure site symbols.

Why is this important? These are symbols that we've been trained to accept as trustworthy, reliable, and stable. By including them, you are reassuring your prospect that your site shares the same qualities.

Remember, the number-one fear prospects have when they come to your selling website is that you might rip them off. They're going to give you their credit card information even though they're not certain what you'll do with it.

In most cases, they've never met you. They don't know that much about you, so there is a measure of fear in this process. Everything you can do to remove that fear is vitally important to closing more sales. So use the credit card logos, which are familiar and trusted icons in our society, and include your guarantee. This is all inside the offer box.

We're going to talk more about the guarantee on its own, but now I'm talking about including the guarantee inside the offer box and also the Better Business Bureau logo if you are authorized to use it.

> **Give them every opportunity to succeed at giving you money.**

7) Use *both* an order *button* and a *text link* (such as "click to order").

I prefer the html order button for one simple reason. It works and looks right in all browsers, which may or may not be the case for a graphic icon or button. So why do I recommend you use *both* the button and a text link? It's always best to assume that your user or reader doesn't really know with 100 percent certainty what to do next. Give them every opportunity to succeed at giving you money.

8) Do not sleepwalk through the guarantee.

The guarantee is also known as the "risk reversal" section of your copy. Why do we call it risk reversal? As we said earlier, the biggest fear prospects have when they come to your website is the fear that you are going to rip them off.

You want to reassure them—as much as possible—that the decision they're making is the right decision and that they cannot make a mistake. That's what the "risk reversal" section is all about. This is where you make it clear to them you're taking the risk off their shoulders and placing it squarely on your own shoulders.

If you don't believe this is true, I'd like you to think about something: If someone orders your product or service and he or she is not satisfied with it and asks for a refund, you have to ship the refund back to him or her and he or she has to ship the product back to you. Who was the loser in the transaction? If you require your buyer to pay all the shipping and so forth, you might think you haven't really lost anything … but you have.

At the very least, you've lost the time and energy it took to fulfill the order, to deal with the refund request, to make the refund, and then to restock your item. Haven't you then taken the risk away from your buyer and taken it upon yourself?

By offering a guarantee, aren't you really saying, "I'm willing to stand by the quality of my product or service, and I'm so confident of the quality of that product or service that I'm willing to take the risk of giving you a guarantee even though you might choose to send my product back"?

I choose to think of it like this: Even though I know my product is top quality and delivers more than I promise in my sales letters and communications, I know that some people—for whatever reason—will choose to not honor our transaction and will request a refund (perhaps even after copying the material I've sent them!). They may even order my product, never open it, and then right before the guarantee period is ending, send it back to me quickly. I feel they have dishonored our transaction by not opening the material, looking at it, or reviewing it, or by deciding ahead of time that they were just going to order the material, copy it, and send me back the information.

Even though I believe that kind of behavior is dishonorable, I'm still willing to honor the guarantee, because the truth is, if you do your job in the sales copy and you do your job delivering your product or service, the number of people who will rip you off by requesting a refund is very small.

I really want you to get—deep in your bones—the fact that *risk reversal* is exactly what it says. It's not some semantic trick of language; it truly is reversal of risk.

Don't sleepwalk through writing your risk reversal or guarantee section. Don't just write "100% money back guarantee." I think you should offer that, but it's important to give it an extra dimension. Describe your guarantee in fresh unique ways. We're going to look at guarantees in-depth in the next chapter.

9) Put your risk reversal inside a certificate.

This creates credibility, and it increases conversions. Putting something in certificate form lends it credibility. I know from testing that putting the risk reversal or guarantee inside a certificate increases conversions. It just works.

10) Keep selling, *especially* in the risk reversal section.

This is a perfect place to restate the benefits of your offer. People are going to look at your guarantee. It's quite possible it'll be one of the few things they actually read on your page before making a buying decision.

It's an opportunity for you to restate your benefits. How do you do this? It's a very simple technique. Just describe the benefits in your guarantee or risk reversal language.

Let me give you an example. "Order my e-book, read every page. If you're not delighted with the results, if in fact you don't lose at least 30 pounds in 30 days, find it easy to eat the right foods without feeling hungry or deprived, know in an instant what you're supposed to eat without ever having to refer to a calorie chart or point system, then I refuse to keep your money."

See what I did? Didn't I just restate the benefits in that sentence, which was part of a guarantee? You can do the same, and you should. Keep selling even in your guarantee section.

11) Use "100 percent money back"" language, but don't rely on that to convey the message of your guarantee.

Use active language to dimensionalize your guarantee. I've already described this, but pay attention to this step carefully.

I do believe you should include the "100 percent money back guarantee" language. Some people simply look for that phrase as their assurance that there are no tricks involved in your guarantee. For some, it's important that you use that specific language in your guarantee. Use it, but don't make that the only guarantee you offer; be more descriptive.

12) Add video to your risk reversal section.

Make your risk reversal or guarantee personal, persuasive, and passionate. One of the best ways you can do that is by using the human voice and face, especially if your personality is part of your marketing. A video of you personally delivering the guarantee is more powerful than text alone.

13) Use your signature in the risk reversal section.

It increases conversions. Why? If it's signed, we feel like it's a deal; it's official; it's a contract. If I put my signature on something, I'm making a statement that says I identify with this guarantee, with this product, or with this risk reversal. My word is my bond, and here's my signature to prove it.

Some people are concerned about using their actual signature online. There are a number of solutions to that problem. First, you can have someone else sign so the signature would be distinct from your own. Then, there would never be a problem with forgery. You can also use handwriting software that generates handwritten text that appears to be real but isn't your real signature.

I recommend against using the handwritten fonts that you have in MS Word. They're not very convincing. People have seen them before, and they will know that's not your signature. When people look for a signature, they want to see a real signature from a real person.

So if you're going to use a software or handwriting font solution, then I recommend you invest in a good one. Use your signature and sign the deal, which leads to …

14) Use a handwritten guarantee.

If a signature works, a handwritten guarantee often works even better. Handwritten guarantees have been shown time and again to authenticate the guarantee in the reader's mind and increase conversion dramatically.

If you're going to use a handwritten guarantee, make sure that it's short, powerful, and most important, legible. Nothing is worse than a guarantee where the handwriting is so bad you can't read it.

15) The "close" is you asking for the order.

This is where you're asking for the sale, the order. You're taking their money and giving them the product in exchange. In chapter 8 we will explore closing copy more in-depth.

16) Use all the tools that are available to you at the close.

That means you want a headline on the order page just as I described: one that's affirmative, congratulatory, and lets them know they've made the right decision. You want to recap all the major benefits, probably the same ones you had listed in your offer box on the sales letter page. Restate your guarantee or your risk reversal.

You want to use urgency, scarcity, and reward. Urgency and scarcity can be accomplished by setting limits. Set a time limit: "You must order by Friday at 5:00;" or a numerical limit: "We only have 13 of these kits available. You must order before they're all gone;" or a date limit based on a sale's expiration. If you can introduce some urgency into the selling process ethically and honestly, then you should do it.

For a reward, you might offer, "For the next 10 people who order this product, we will also give you a special report on ...," or "... we'll give you a second gizmo," or whatever the appropriate bonus offer might be. That rewards fast action. Make sure you're offering a limited number or a limited time on your bonus items, and make certain it's all honest and ethical.

Make your promotions real, honest, and ethical.

Nothing can hurt your credibility more than if you say, "We will offer this bonus only until Friday at 12:00 noon!" Then your reader comes back Friday at 1:00 p.m. to see if you were lying or not and discovers that, in fact, you were lying. In fact, you've changed the date on the website using a sneaky little script.

Don't resort to those kinds of tricks. Make your promotions real, honest, and ethical. You will be rewarded in return.

17) Tell your reader what to do to close the deal.

This is where you need to be as specific as possible. In fact, you might even feel as though you're writing to a third grader. You're going to use language like this: "Okay, now's the time to type in your name and your address, double-check that the information is correct, then type in your credit card number and click on the 'Buy now' button."

You want to be just that specific in your instructions. If you can give these instructions in audio or video, that's even better.

18) You want to reassure and praise your readers.

Everyone craves affirmation. Give them what they want. If you've created a truly useful product or service that makes a difference in the lives of buyers, you should have no shame in saying, "I'm so proud of you for making this decision to buy my product or service, and I'm so excited about the difference it's going to make in your life. I can't wait to hear your success story, and I do hope you'll share it with me. Here's what you should do right now, type in your name, address, and credit card information and click the button that says 'Buy now,' so I can rush your items to you right away."

Reassure and praise your reader for the good decision he or she made.

19) Explain what's going to happen.

Tell them exactly what's going to happen when they press the "Submit" or "Buy now" button. This is a question your reader is wondering about. "When I click on this, am I going to get a printable receipt? Am I going to be taken to a download page? What's going to happen when I click that button?"

The best way to reassure them is to tell them what's going to happen or even show them if you can make a screen capture video that shows exactly what's going to happen. Have a message or arrow pointing to the video that says, "Click here to watch a video about what happens next."

You could have audio that plays, saying, "When you click the 'Buy now' button, you'll be taken to a page where you can immediately download your items, and you can also print out your receipt and proof of purchase on the next page. Go ahead and click the 'Buy now' button now."

20) Maintain the look and feel of your website.

Your order form should look exactly like your website. In many cases, the order form will be hosted somewhere other than your own server. Usually, it will be hosted through the shopping cart system.

There is a problem, however, when the order page looks entirely different from your actual website. Unconsciously, your buyers will feel there's a disconnect between what you're telling them and what you're selling them.

Make the transition seamless. When people enroll in my Copywriting Academy Coaching Program, they probably don't even notice when they go from clicking on the order button to getting to the download or access page that they actually switch servers two times. That's by design. We made sure the pages look exactly the same when you make that transition. You should do the same—keep the look and feel identical.

There is a phenomenon I call the Instantaneous Subconscious Association (ISA). This simply means your readers are noticing the look and feel of your website, and if it's inconsistent, they feel that *you* are inconsistent—that your *business* is inconsistent.

How do we feel about people in our lives who are not consistent? How do you feel about a business or institution that treats you in an *inconsistent* manner? Don't you feel you can't rely on them; that you can't *trust* them to behave in a certain way? You don't want your readers, prospects, or buyers to feel that way about you, so don't give them a reason to.

21) Test your order form.

Sometimes it's the simplest things that can trip up your shopping cart system. If you haven't tested it before your Web visitors use it, you could potentially be in for some embarrassing and costly problems.

Order your own product. If it's an expensive product and you want to minimize your processing expense, set it to zero dollars or one dollar and make multiple orders. Try to break your order form; try to put in erroneous information. Think about what your prospects might do on your order page that could possibly trip up your system and then do those things and see what happens.

It's better if you know in advance, rather than discover it when you get that complaint call from an unhappy buyer or when you watch sales trickle through your fingers because your order form didn't work properly.

Many times I find that clients and companies don't even realize they're losing orders. This is where many orders are lost, at the actual order page in the shopping cart. Make sure you have a backup plan. What's going to happen if the customer's credit card is declined or the transaction doesn't go through? Do you call him or her? Is the customer taken to a different Web page? Think about what happens next in that process and plan for it. Recover from declined cards and abandoned shopping carts and you will increase sales.

In the next chapter, we deep-dive on writing powerful guarantees.

---------------------------------☞---------------------------------

CHAPTER 6 QUICK SUMMARY:

21 Steps to Irresistible Offers, Rock-Solid Risk Reversal, and Powerful Closes

1. **Make Your Offer "Stand Alone."** If the offer section is the only part your prospect reads—can he or she make a buying decision?

2. **Apply the P.A.S.T.O.R. Formula to Your Offer.** Invoke attention, interest, desire, and a call to action.

3. **Enclose your order area copy in a differentiating text box.** Make it stand apart from the rest of the copy.

4. **Use the Prospect's Positive Voice in the Offer.** Give the prospect the words to say inside his or her own mind.

5. **Use Aspirational Language**. Focus on the outcome your reader desires.

6. **Use Credit Card Logos and Secure Site Symbols.** Reassure your prospect with these familiar icons; also include your guarantee and the BBB logo (if you are authorized to do so).

7. **Use an Order Button AND a Text Link.** Make it easy and obvious how you wish the reader to proceed.

8. **Do Not Sleepwalk Through the Guarantee.** This is the biggest mistake made with the risk reversal section.

9. **Put Your Risk Reversal Inside a Certificate.** This creates credibility and increases conversions.

10. **Keep Selling—Especially in the Risk Reversal Section.** State your benefits as part of the guarantee.

11. **Use "100% Money-Back," but Don't Rely on It.** Use active language to dimensionalize your guarantee.

12. **Add Video to Your Risk Reversal Section.** Make it personal, persuasive, and passionate.

13. **Use Your Signature in the Risk Reversal Section.** Increases conversions.

14. **Use a Handwritten Guarantee.** Handwritten guarantees can work very well when *you* are the product.

15. **The Close Is You Asking For the Order.** Until they press "Submit," you don't have an order.

16. **Use All Available Tools at the Close.** Benefits, guarantee, audio, video, urgency, scarcity, and reward.

17. **Tell Your Reader What to Do to Close the Deal.** Be as specific as possible.

18. **Reassure and Praise Your Reader.** Everyone craves affirmation; give it to them.

19. **Explain What's Going to Happen.** Tell them exactly what will happen when they press "Submit."

20. **Maintain Look and Feel.** Your order form should look like your website.

21. **Test Your Order Form!** Try to "break" it. Have a backup plan. Recover from "declines" and "abandons"; increase sales.

---

*Claim **your FREE membership** (retail value $197) including a growing library of templates & tutorials, visit CopyThatSellsBook.com (no credit card required).*

7

HOW TO WRITE GUARANTEES THAT DISSOLVE FEAR AND UNLEASH A RIVER OF SALES

"A promise made is a debt unpaid."
—Robert W. Service

L et's review. What have you already done? If you've worked your way through this book carefully, you already understand your buyers, what motivates them, what are their fears, frustrations and anxieties. Not only that…

- You know the language they use to talk about their problem.
- You know the product you're selling them.
- You know what the benefits of the products are that the prospect cares about.
- You've developed a "big idea," or Copy Thesis™ that sums up why they want this product.
- You've established and verified (with a preponderance of proof) that your solution works.

- You've crafted powerful bullet points that appeal to every possible tiny variation of every benefit, and answering every objection before it's raised.
- You've written a magnetic headline and subheads that draw people into and through your copy with momentum.
- You've stacked the building blocks of your sales letter so they ultimately buy your product or idea.

You've done all this amazing persuasion work and yet... it's still not enough. Why?

Fear.

We need to remove fear, so that people are free to buy. Before we do that, we have to understand where this fear comes from.

In any transaction, there is risk on both sides. If you're a product creator and you've sold any products at all before, any training, coaching or consulting, you already know there's risk on your part. You could end up with a "dud" client. "Dud" clients include those who don't pay what they owe, or those who are energy or time vampires, or perhaps they're even just weird and creepy.

There are so many different ways that people can *take* from you, even if they are a customer.

Further, there's the risk that some people will buy from you and then rip you off... download your materials and ask for a refund, which they intended to do from the beginning. In the credit card world they call it "friendly fraud." I'm not sure what's friendly about it.

There's a definite risk involved for you, when you accept anyone as a client.

There is, of course, also risk for the buyer. Their risk is that they might not get what they paid for. Put yourself in the buyer's position. What are *you* afraid of when you purchase a program, product or service?

You're afraid you won't get what you paid for. You're afraid it won't be the way it was represented.

You're afraid it might work for *other* people but it won't work for *you*. The buyer's safest default position is to **not believe you** without proof. It's in their best interest is to begin the relationship not believing you.

DON'T DESPAIR – THEY'RE SECRETLY ON YOUR SIDE

I know the picture I've painted so far seems rather pessimistic. But inside all this fear, there's actually very good news. There's a secret you need to know about your prospects. Here's the secret… when they visit your sales page, or your website… when they come to your seminar, your retreat, etc… they secretly **want you to be right**.

They secretly **want** to buy from you.

They secretly **hope you have the solution**.

The challenge is, they also know it's in their best interest to not believe any of that upfront. That's why you need proof, but even "mere proof" is not enough.

You must convey the idea that **you** are shouldering most of the risk. If you can transfer the risk from the buyer to yourself, that removes the barrier, it removes the fear and they're free to do what they most want to do – buy your product.

Armed with this knowledge, you can sell from confidence. You have so much confidence in what you're offering that you are willing to bet on it. You're going to put *your* money on the line. You're going to "put your money where your mouth is."

HOW DO YOU CONVEY THIS MESSAGE?

1. *First, you have to* <u>be</u> *this message. You have to really* <u>feel</u> *this way.* In the case of the Copywriting Academy Program (<u>WriteCopyThatSells. com</u>), I believe in my heart that it's one of the best, if not the best,

copywriting training programs for entrepreneurs in existence. I'm willing to bet on it and I offered the program with a 30-day guarantee that you could get your money back if it doesn't work for you. I take a lot of risk in that because what I'm betting on is that you'll get the power of the idea so deeply in your bones, in your DNA that you'll actually do the work to put this to work so you can see if it works for you or not.

The program/product that I'm offering in this training is one that requires work on your part, it's not just a pill that you take that works magic on your physiological body. It's not just something that you stick into your gas tank that gives you more gas mileage. It's not something that you can read and learn and automatically benefit from it, you have to work at it. I have to be willing to bet on you, and you need to come from the same place when you're thinking about your product or service.

2. Second, you offer proof and credibility.

We've talked about how you do that, how you present proof in the form of testimonials and credibility in the form of other accomplishments or the form of people that you worked for or with, things that you've accomplished. Of course, you need to offer a money back guarantee.

If you're taking payment via credit cards, you're required to offer a money back guarantee. It's part of your contract with the credit card merchant provider. If customers aren't satisfied with your service or product, you must refund their money. If the merchant provider thinks too many people have asked for a refund, they will revoke your credit card merchant account.

So you really have to be willing to bet on it and you have to go further than offering just a money back guarantee. You need to offer that, because you're required to, but you also need to go beyond it. You have to deal with all the risks that the buyer is taking. You have to convince them, to show them, to demonstrate to them that you are the one taking the risk.

Now, let me assure you that the thing they're most afraid of isn't necessarily losing their money. Of course, nobody wants to lose money, but there are things that buyers hate more than losing money. I'll tell you what some of those things are.

- **They hate hassle more than they fear losing money.**

If they think they'll have to go through a lot of bureaucratic red tape to get their money back, sometimes they just let it go. Some unethical companies count on that as part of their business strategy. I implore you not to be that kind of company, because that's just dirty. Make it easy and hassle-free for people to get their money back, and make that message clear to them. You may find this hard to believe, but buyers often hate the hassle more than they fear losing their money.

- **Buyers hate stress more than they fear losing money.**

Most of us have enough stress in our lives already; we certainly don't want to take on more. We don't want to deal with pushy salespeople. We don't want to deal with rude customer service reps. We don't want to worry about the purchase we're making. We don't want our spouse to think we made a stupid buying decision. If you give your customers any hint that dealing with you will ever be stressful, they may avoid doing business with you at all.

- **Buyers hate looking foolish more than they fear losing money.**

This happens often with weight loss programs. People see the before and after pictures and they think they're going to look like that. They get the program, they talk about it to everyone they know and become evangelists for the program. Have you ever known anyone who acted this way? Then, maybe they lost weight at first and a few weeks later they put all the weight back on ... and they feel foolish.

Maybe you know someone who's had that experience, or maybe you've had that experience yourself. The specter of looking foolish looms in the background of your prospect's mind.

- **Buyers hate _feeling_ foolish even more than _looking_ foolish.**

Prospects also don't like to feel foolish. None of us likes to feel we have been duped or taken advantage of. Buyers hate this more than losing money.

YOUR GUARANTEE MUST DISPEL FEAR

Your guarantee (or risk-reversal) has to not only guarantee their money back, but it must dispel fear.

You must overcome the prospect's fear by showing them that you are the one taking the risk.

I have a very specific method for doing just that. I call it "Ray's Way" of writing a 10-part guarantee that will multiply your sales.

This is the next level, beyond "mere money back guarantees." A money back guarantee is good, but it's language that's been used so often that it almost becomes wallpaper. We expect it, it's going to be there, but it feels meaningless.

We want to know that there _is_ one (a money-back guarantee), but I think half the time we don't believe the company will actually give us our money back. Or we believe it will be too much stress and hassle for us to bother with it…, or we'll look so foolish and stupid we don't even want to talk to anybody about it. The plain old "money back guarantee" has become a lot less effective than it once was.

You *must* use the language, "money back guarantee" in your sales copy, but it's not enough. You have to go beyond it. If you use my way of writing a 10-part guarantee, it'll increase your sales. It'll decrease your refunds, because people will be more deeply committed to their decision than they would be otherwise.

It also increases the lifetime average value of a customer, because if they're satisfied with one purchase, then they'll likely make another purchase, and another. Every time they make additional purchases, they become more valuable over the lifetime of their relationship with you.

Does that sound like good stuff you'd like to have happen? Let's get going. Here's how to construct a 10-part guarantee that is powerful beyond belief.

1. Start with the words "100% unconditional money back guarantee"

Wait a minute, Ray! You just told me that doesn't work. No, I said it's not *enough*. You definitely need to have it because for some people this is the only code they will accept on your sales page that means they're protected. If they don't see these "code words" they won't accept that you are safe.

2. Sell your benefits and transformation in the guarantee itself

Don't worry I'm going to explain how to do this, I won't just give you the abstract description of, do all this and good luck. I'll show you how to do it because we're going to write a guarantee.

3. Integrate your USP (unique selling proposition) into the language of the guarantee itself

Have you ever heard anybody teach this? I'm sure you've heard people talk about making a guarantee and making sure it's unconditional and that there's no hassle. Maybe you even put your signature at the bottom so they feel you're personally guaranteeing it. But, have you ever heard anybody teach that in the guarantee itself you need to sell your benefits and transformation? That in the guarantee itself you need to integrate your USP? You might have, but it's unlikely because most people, even copywriters or direct response marketers, aren't aware they should be doing this.

A few are, but this is rarely used, and even more rarely understood. So if you'll internalize this and start practicing it, this alone is worth about one thousand times your investment in this book.

4. Personalize the guarantee

This means more than just putting something that looks like your signature at the bottom of the guarantee. Convey the idea that this isn't just an impersonal company guarantee, but that it's your personal promise. It's your own integrity you're putting on the line.

5. Give the longest guarantee possible

If you can give longer than 30 days, then do it. Your credit card processor may not like it, and you may have to negotiate with them on this, but my testing has proven to my satisfaction that in almost every case, the longer the guarantee the lower the refund rate.

6. Demonstrate that returns are easy and hassle-free

Don't just describe it, but show it. Prove it.

7. Assure them that this is a no-strings attached, unconditional guarantee

Sometimes it's appropriate to offer a conditional guarantee. There are instances in which that's a good thing to do, depending on the investment the customer makes in your program and your cost of delivering the service or training. Most of the time, though, in almost all cases, you should offer a no-strings attached, unconditional guarantee.

8. Emphasize the speed of refunds

People may believe that you're going to honor their refund request. They may believe it will be a relatively hassle-free process, but even if they have those things settled in their mind, they probably still suspect it'll take them weeks to get the check.

9. Amaze them with what I call the "I'll-take-the-risk twist."

This one takes some backbone, but if you have the stamina to do it, this will ramp up your sales like crazy. In this instance, you might offer to send them double their money back. Or to send them their money back, and let them keep the product... or some other outrageous promise that makes it clear that you have absolute faith in the quality of your product.

10. Give your guarantee a name

It can't be "the guarantee," it has to have a *special* name. An evocative, descriptive, differentiating name. One that makes it stand out from other, "inferior" guarantees. Something like, "Our Super-Strong, Good as Gold Fort Knox Guarantee"... or "The World-Famous Double Your Money Back, No Questions Asked, No Weasel Guarantee."

...

That's "Ray's Way" of constructing a 10- part guarantee that has power, and that will boost the sales of your product or service. If I were you, my next question would be, *how do I do all that?*

That's a great question. In the following pages, you get to watch me transform a weak, lily-livered guarantee into an iron-clad deal maker.

THE AMAZING TRANSFORMATION OF A WEAK GUARANTEE INTO THE INCREDIBLE HULK OF RISK REVERSAL

Let's start with this... a sad little guarantee, a weakling, one who's always bullied on the playground, always getting sand kicked in his face and never making a sale because he's not much of a guarantee.

This is a guarantee for an imaginary dentist. We'll call him Dr. Ben Parker. Maybe he has a cosmetic dentistry makeover service that makes your smile look better, and here's his guarantee...

Dr. Ben Parker's cosmetic dentistry makeover comes with a 100% satisfaction guarantee. You are pleased with what we do for you or we will make it right, guaranteed.

You might say, "Well, that's not so bad."

You're right, it's not so bad. It's at least average, maybe even better than average, but it's not going to inspire the kind of confidence we need to get buyers to believe that we're taking on all the risk. It is a sad, sad little guarantee.

Let's go to work on this using the same product, but changing the guarantee. It means having some backbone, some belief in what you offer. I'm going to pretend that Dr. Ben Parker is my client and he's told me, "Ray, whatever you have to do to make my guarantee work, to get more people to come to my clinic, and get this makeover, do it. I'll back up the guarantee you create, because I believe in my product. I believe in it so much I'm willing to bet on it."

I smile. "Dr. Parker," I say, "Let's do this thing."

TOTAL GUARANTEE MAKEOVER

First, let's rewrite the guarantee to sell the benefits. Thus:

> *Dr. Ben Parker's cosmetic dentistry makeover, comes with a 100%
> money back guarantee.* **You will see yourself with the beautiful
> straight teeth of a movie star. Your friends will envy the
> brilliant, flawless, whiteness of your new million-watt smile,
> and your new smile will look 100% natural, all in just one
> painless visit.** *You'll be pleased with what we do for you or we will
> make it right, guaranteed.*

Of course, I don't think there is a cosmetic dentistry makeover that
can be done in one visit, but just for the purposes of example I'm going
a bit overboard. You can adopt this to whatever your actual situation
is, and maybe I'm wrong and there *is* a dentist that will do this in one
visit. One *painless* visit I'm not sure about, but if you're that dentist...
contact me.

The next step is to integrate your USP.

What *is* your unique selling proposition? Let's pretend that Dr.
Ben Parker's USP, the thing that makes him stand out, is he's known as
"Painless Parker, the world's gentlest dentist."

Back in the 1800s, there actually *was* a dentist known as Painless
Parker, and he was quite the marketer. He was well-known and not always
revered, because he was seen by his colleagues as a snake-oil salesman.
That doesn't change the fact that he *was* known as Painless Parker and
his patients *loved* him. I don't know how he managed to do that. Maybe
he gave them opiates, filled them up with liquor, or hypnotized them...
but somehow he managed to live up to his "painless" reputation. He had
a very successful business as a result.

Let's pretend that our modern day Dr. Parker has more acceptable
means of making his dentistry painless. Maybe he uses neuro feedback

techniques, hypnotic induction or even some light anesthetics or a combination of these things, but somehow he manages to make his dentistry painless and gentle, and that's his USP. The copy then reads…

> *Dr. Ben Parker's cosmetic dentistry makeover, comes with a 100% money back guarantee. You will see yourself with the beautiful straight teeth of a movie star. Your friends will envy the brilliant, flawless, whiteness of your new million-watt smile, and your new smile will look 100% natural, all in just one painless visit. **There's a good reason he's known as "Painless Parker, the World's Gentlest Dentist".***

Our next step would be to personalize the guarantee with Dr. Ben Parker's signature, and add language like, "I take your smile very seriously and you have my personal promise…" I would actually use Dr. Parker's real signature if this was a real client.

Then we want to give the longest possible guarantee. In this case I'll have Dr. Parker guarantee his work for life. Your credit card merchant account may not allow you to give a lifetime guarantee or they may not let you give more than a 90-day guarantee and in some cases you can't give more than 30 days, so you may need to take an alternative form of payment in order to offer longer guarantees.

I can tell you that even though it feels riskier, I have much experience with offering longer guarantees. I have one client in particular, has a standard one year guarantee on his products. People can buy them and benefit from them, and return them up to a year later for a full, no questions asked refund. His refund rate is quite low. I think it's because the one-year guarantee alleviates a lot of fear and pressure from people's minds. Maybe these customers are thinking, "Well, if they're behind it for a full year it *must* be good."

Will some people take advantage of this because they need Christmas shopping money next year? Yes, a few will, and that's just the cost of doing business. In the long run, I think you'll make more sales and ultimately you'll make more profit by offering the longest guarantee possible.

The next step is to show that returns are easy and aren't going to be a problem.

You need to go into some detail about this and you can see below in my finished rewrite, I've added more copy, making it obvious how you might ask for a refund of Dr. Parker's services. We have a phone number for them to call. Also on the page with the guarantee is a mailing address and an email, all the different ways people can contact Dr. Parker's office to get their refund.

The next step is to make sure that you emphasize there are no strings attached.

You do that in the copy as I've done at the bottom and I use very fancy, sophisticated language. I *say there are absolutely no strings attached, no forms to fill out, nothing to prove, etc.* Look at this copy in context below as we finish adding the different pieces to the guarantee.

The next step is where we talk about the *speed* of the refund.

We want them to know they won't have to wait forever, so it's very simple. At the bottom you can see I've written, *"and you won't have to wait, we will issue your refund check on the spot."*

Then we amaze them.

How, you might ask, can you be more amazing than offering the refund on the spot?

By saying that Dr. Parker is so confident in his work, he's so sure you'll be overwhelmed with gratitude that he will give you **double your money back**. This is clearly daring and you need to believe in your product very strongly before being able to offer this, but there are many companies who offer a double your money back guarantee and, in some cases, triple your money back.

They do it because they know they can deliver what they promise. Now, if you can deliver what you promise and you're willing to do this to back it up, this will make your guarantee almost irresistible.

The final step is to name the guarantee, but I'm not sharing the name with you until we do the final comparison. I came up with a pretty good name for it.

Let's start by looking again at the sad little guarantee from the beginning.

Sad Little Guarantee

Dr. Ben Parker's cosmetic dentistry makeover, comes with a 100% satisfaction guarantee. You are pleased with what we do for you or we will make it right, guaranteed.

Okay, not bad but not great. Let's look at the Ray's Way version and see if it's any different.

Dr. Parker's Love-Your-New-Smile, or Double-Your-Money-Back, No-Hassle Lifetime Guarantee

Dr. Ben Parker's cosmetic dentistry makeover, comes with a 100% money-back guarantee... but we don't stop there. We promise you will see yourself with the beautiful straight teeth of a movie star. Your friends will envy the brilliant, flawless whiteness of your new million-watt smile, and your new smile will look 100% natural, all in just one painless visit. There's a good reason he's known as Painless Parker, the World's Gentlest Dentist. Here's a note from Dr. Parker himself:

"I take your smile very seriously, and you have my personal promise that I will not rest until you are dazzled and delighted by

your new smile. Transform smiles, transform lives. I believe in my work so much, I guarantee it for life." - Dr. Ben Parker

At any time, if you decide Dr. Parker hasn't just performed a miracle on that dull, discolored, uneven smile of yours, transforming it into the beautiful perfect smile of your dreams, just call 555-111-1212 and tell any of our staff — or even Dr. Parker himself, if you like — and we'll give you a complete refund. You can also email or send your request by postal mail to the postal address below or even just stop by.

*If you aren't satisfied we would not feel right keeping your money, so we make it easy to get a refund. And just to be clear, there are absolutely no strings attached, no forms to fill out, nothing to prove and we promise we won't question you. **We won't even ask for the teeth back.** Just for the record, we've done 1,135 of these procedures and haven't had one single refund request.*

And you won't have to wait either, we will issue any refund check on the spot. In fact, Dr. Parker is so confident in his work and so sure you'll be overwhelmed with gratitude for your new smile, and your new life, that we're making this promise... anyone who requests a refund will receive, without question, hassle or any delay, double your money back!

That, my friends, is a guarantee.

CHAPTER 7 QUICK SUMMARY:

Ray's Way 10-Part Guarantee Formula

1. **Start with the words "100% unconditional money back guarantee."** For some people this is required "code language" that signals they are safe in making the transaction.

2. **Sell your benefits and transformation in the guarantee itself.** This is an opportunity to reinforce the desire the prospect has for the benefits they desire.

3. **Integrate your USP (unique selling proposition) into the language of the guarantee itself.** The very qualities that make you and your offer unique and appealing should be woven into your guarantee.

4. **Personalize the guarantee.** Make it more than a guarantee – make it a personal promise from the company spokesperson, or business persona.

5. **Give the longest guarantee possible.** Tests have shown that longer guarantees result in lower refund rates.

6. **Demonstrate that returns are easy and hassle-free.** Remove the fears and misgivings people have about how tough it will be to get a refund if they want one.

7. **Assure them that this is a no-strings attached, unconditional guarantee.** It's easy to deal with the very well-known assumptions customers have about the "hassle factor."

8. **Emphasize the speed of refunds.** Show that refunds will happen very quickly.

9. **Amaze them with what I call the "I'll-take-the-risk twist."** Show the prospect that you, not they, are shouldering the risk.

10. **Give your guarantee a name.** Naming it makes it real, makes it unique, and differentiates your guarantee from those of your competitors.

---

*Claim **your FREE membership** (retail value $197) including a growing library of templates & tutorials, visit CopyThatSellsBook.com (no credit card required).*

8

HOW TO WRITE COPY
THAT CLOSES THE DEAL

"Timid salesmen have skinny kids."
—Zig Ziglar

Closing the deal.

Writing copy that closes the sale.

It's not the exact same thing as in selling face-to-face, although it does serve the same purpose... and that is to ask for the sale.

There are a bunch of things that happen in the close that you may not be aware of or may not realize are part of your closing copy.

First, recap the offer.

Retell the story of what you're selling. Maybe this is the only part of the copy they read. Maybe they just need to be reminded of the benefits. You want to be sure to forge the chain of logic you use to make it reasonable to them that they should buy your offer.

Don't take forever. Don't take the same amount of time that you took to write out the chain of logic in your body copy, but you do want to recap the logical series of decisions they would need to make in order to make the decision to buy.

And certainly, in your closing copy, drive home the benefits and the "big reason why," that would make them buy this thing to begin with. You want to reconnect to the outcome that had them interested in the beginning.

Remind them of the guarantee and the bonuses. You don't have to go into great detail, but do mention them.

Your job is only to elicit a decision. "Yes" is a valid answer, and so is "no." You don't want them to be in decision purgatory, which is called "maybe." Maybe is the worst place for them to be. You don't want them in "no man's land." You want them to either say yes or no.

Finally, the most important thing in your closing copy is that you must ask for the sale.

This is the biggest failure in face-to-face sales, believe it or not. People will spend hours prospecting, setting an appointment up with someone and making a sales presentation, preparing it and presenting, and then not even ask for the sale in the face-to-face sales encounter.

Why? Well, the number one answer is probably because we're afraid of rejection. However, if you want to succeed in selling face-to-face, you have to learn to ask for the sale. You have to overcome that fear and the same is true in online sales, although the funny thing is it's not nearly as scary, because you're not looking them in the eye, so I'm not sure why people hesitate. But they do.

Don't fail to ask for the sale.

Also, this is the biggest failure in most advertising. How many ads have you seen that never really ask you to come into the store or make a purchase?

It's certainly the biggest failure in sales copy. For some reason people take a step back when it's time to ask for the sale. I don't know why, other than the innate fear of rejection. Like I said, if you're writing sales copy you're not there in person for the rejection — so what does it matter, just ask for the sale!

Don't fail to ask for the sale. That's the key to remember about closing sales copy.

5 CLOSING TEMPLATES THAT GET THE JOB DONE

Your closing copy doesn't have to be long or complicated, but it *does* need to be effective. I have found that metaphors seem to work best. You'll see what I mean as I walk you through these five closing templates.

These are the five templates I use most often when writing copy and they work the best for me, so I go back to them time and time again, because they never fail.

You'll see how easily you can adapt these templates to your own usage as we go through them.

Your **transitional copy** moves the reader out of the main sales copy and into the close. It comes after the guarantee, the bonuses, the pricing, etc. and rolls into the final closing paragraphs or sentences of the sales page. Here's an example:

TRANSITIONAL CLOSING COPY (USE WITH EACH OF THE 5 CLOSING TEMPLATES)

Anyone can pay off their mortgage 10 years early using the Provantage No-Fail Debt Reduction System. I've shown you the proof that it works for me, for others, and it will work for you too. You know that with the 90-day no way to lose, double your money back guarantee, you are 100% protected and safe.

You can see that I've reconnected to the benefits. I've restated the big idea. I've reminded them of the guarantee … and then I move on to **the closing metaphor**.

1. *"You Will Certainly Arrive" Close*

Here's what you and I both know, one year from today you will certainly arrive. The question is where? That is your decision to make right now.

Then you simply end your sales letter. This is a template for using a metaphor that helps people understand the need to go ahead and make a decision right now.

The metaphor is, *we both know you're going to arrive, the question is where?* I purposefully leave that question open for *them* to answer. It's more powerful that way.

2. *The "Different Results" Close*

I have the same transition copy as before, followed by…

Here's the tough truth you probably already know. If you want different results you need to do something different. Make a definitive decision right now to get different results.

Then you can either put a buy button here, or close out your copy and whatever language is appropriate for your offer.

3. *The "Crossroads" Close*

The same transition copy, again, leading into…

You're standing at the crossroads. To the left is the same rough, rocky road you've been traveling. To the right is the road fewer people will choose. This road is not harder it's different. Choosing the right road makes all the difference. I'm hoping you'll choose the right road and join us today.

Now, this template is powerful because it plays on some famous language that's deeply embedded in our subconscious, which is from the poem by Robert Frost called *The Road Not Taken*.

I don't actually quote that, but I use language that is evocative of it and also, I chose to make the *right* road also happen to be the *correct* road. Choosing the *right* road makes all the difference. Choose the *right* road and join us today. While that's not very subtle, it is indicative of the direction that we want them to go, and that in fact they themselves want to go – or else they wouldn't still be reading.

4. The "Decision Time" Close

This is much more straightforward. Again, we have the transition copy and then we simply say...

> *It's been said that in your moments of decision your destiny is shaped. What will you decide to do right now? The same thing you've been doing so you get the same old results or will you decide to change your results for the better by joining the Champion Circle...*

...or whatever the name of your club, training or program is.

5. The "Handholding" Close

Again, using the transition copy followed by...

> *And you won't be alone, I'm going to hold your hand every step of the way and walk you through this process.*

You might even want to spell out the details of how you do that, whether it's on a weekly group coaching calls, one-on-one email coaching, or through the recorded materials and checklists and you're *metaphorically* holding their hand.

Whatever the case may be you want to describe exactly what form the handholding is going to take so they feel reassured, and also so they don't have any false expectations.

CHAPTER 8 QUICK SUMMARY:

5 Closing Copy Templates That Work

1. **The "You Will Certainly Arrive" Close.** The metaphor is, we both know you're going to arrive, the question is where? I purposefully leave that question open for them to answer, I don't answer that for them because I want them to have the answer it's more powerful that way.

2. **The "Different Results" Close.** If you want different results you need to do something different. Make a definitive decision right now to get different results.

3. **The "Crossroads" Close.** This close invokes language that's deeply embedded in our subconscious, which is from the poem by Robert Frost about the road not taken. "I chose the road less traveled, and it has made all the difference."

4. **The "Decision Time" Close.** It's in your moments of decision that your destiny is shaped. What will you decide to do right now?

5. **The "Handholding" Close.** You're metaphorically holding their hand. Show them what that will look like, and be careful that you don't create false expectations.

---

*Claim **your FREE membership** (retail value $197) including a growing library of templates & tutorials, visit CopyThatSellsBook.com (no credit card required).*

9

HOW TO WRITE IRRESISTIBLE OFFERS

"An irresistible offer is one that's so appealing, it sells itself. You don't ask people to buy. They *ask* you.*"*

—Ray Edwards

The Offer is the core of your sales copy. It consists of:

- The benefit of what you're selling (the transformation).
- The vehicle or mechanism that delivers the transformation.
- The price & payment terms.

So what makes an offer "irresistible"? The way in which it is presented.

In this chapter we're going to cover *9 Kinds of Offers.* There are actually more, but these will be plenty to get you started, and will serve you for a long time, because most copywriters and marketers don't even know *these* nine.

So, what *are* the nine offers?

They are simply different ways of structuring the presentation of *what* you're selling and *how* you're selling it. There are advantages and disadvantages to each kind of offer, and I'll be showing you how to choose the offer type best suited for your product or service.

Let's get to it.

OFFER #1 – HARD OFFER

This doesn't mean it's *difficult,* it simply means it's straightforward and there are no fuzzy edges. This is what you get. This is what it will do for you. This is what it costs, so buy it now. It's a hard offer. It's plain.

OFFER #2 – SOFT OFFER

This is the kind of offer that usually involves language like, "Send no money now. We'll send you the kit, shirt, glasses (or whatever) for you to try for 30 days and if you like it we'll automatically bill you."

It's called *soft* because it's easier for the buyer to accept up front. They don't have to pay anything right away, so they're risking nothing. You let them try it for 30 days (or 2 weeks, or 3 months, etc.) and if they keep it, you bill them. The *disadvantage* to this kind of offer is that sometimes the people who accept it somehow "conveniently" forget that you are going to bill them at the end of the trial period, and they get upset. Some will complain to your payment processor, or even file a chargeback.

Keep this in mind. It doesn't matter how clear you are in your explanation, how exacting it is, how large the typeface, I promise you if you do this kind of offer you <u>will</u> get complaints. That doesn't mean you shouldn't do it, (this is a powerful offer that invariably generates a lot of sales)… you simply have to be prepared for the complaints.

OFFER #3 – CHARTER OFFER

This should look familiar to you because you've seen it many times before. It's the first time ever that a product is being offered, and so it's offered at a charter price or rate that nobody will ever get again in the future. There's a certain cutoff date, so if you buy before this particular date and you get the charter rate or VIP early bird rate or what have you, but nobody else ever gets this price again. This only works if you're telling the truth. You can't make this offer more than once, obviously… but you can also stay in "Charter mode" for as long as you want.

OFFER #4 – LIMITED SUPPLY OFFER

This just means there are a specific number of available units or positions.

People often say, it makes no sense to have a "limited supply" in the digital world because you can make as many digital copies as you want. Well you *can*, and you can also release *as few* as you want, so I might only release 100 access passwords to my particular training program, if I don't want everyone on the planet to have it.

Or, maybe I have only 15 places in a class that we're selling. In that case it's a limited number of units or positions that you have available, even if it's digital. Again, like with all these offers, if you're saying that once these are sold it's over, you must be true to your word. You must not be tempted to use the 'limited supply offer' as a bogus ploy

First of all, it's just wrong.

Secondly, it'll get you into a lot of trouble, and eventually your reputation will precede you, and people won't buy from you.

OFFER #5 – LIMITED TIME OFFER

This sounds similar to offer #4, but it's a little different because it's not about the units or positions in the class. In this offer the limitation is that it's good for a specific limited time period. At that particular day and hour the offer is terminated. Again, you have to keep your word, and if you do, this can be powerful.

OFFER #6 – THE APPLICATION OFFER

This is an elite offer. You make people apply for the privilege of buying your product. (Don't laugh, this works like crazy). We use the application offer for our higher-priced workshops, like the Breakthrough Copy Workshop. In this workshop, participants gather with me and my team for three days, and we write their sales letter on the spot. We accept only a few people, and the tuition is $10,000.

But just because you have the ability to write a check doesn't guarantee you have the privilege of getting into the workshop. You have to prove you're a good fit for the group, and that the event is going to be the right thing for you. I don't want someone to come to this if it's not right for them, and I don't want anyone in the room who's going to spoil things for everyone else.

You don't have to be hosting a $10,000 workshop to use this offer. It can be used to sell a position in your online class, in your coaching program or consulting business, etc. This is often a service or a live event, but it can work for nearly any product. You have to make a real application process, you can't just *say* it's an application only process and then not *have* one.

That being said, this offer usually works best for high-ticket items, and it usually involves personal selling. It's very powerful.

OFFER #7 – THE PAYMENT PLAN OFFER

This makes it easier to sell higher ticket items because people don't have to pay all at once up front. It makes the price look more palatable.

This works best for the kinds of offers where you have the power to "turn the faucet off" (for instance, revoke their username and password) if they don't pay.

OFFER #8 – THE ONE-TIME OFFER

You've probably seen this before, it's usually an upsell, or add-on sale.

Usually the copy will say, "This is a one-time offer. You will never see this again."

The key to this offer is that you have to **enforce the limitation**. If it's *really* a one-time offer, you have to go to the trouble of coding the page so that people can't come back to buy it later.

The first few times you do a limited offer, people will ask you to make them the exception to the rule.

Resist the temptation to do that. Let it be known that **you're a person of your word** and when you say it's one-time, there's a time limit, or a deadline... there really is. When you get that reputation, your customers will be quicker to buy when you ask them.

OFFER #9 – THE NEGATIVE OPTION OFFER

It's also known as "forced continuity." The customer buys something and they get a subscription that goes along with the thing they bought. Maybe they buy a set of fitness DVDs and they get an automatic subscription to a "DVD of the month" club, or perhaps they buy a bottle of your nutritional supplement, and then they get a 30-day supply sent to them once a month until they tell you to stop. That's also called "till forbid" billing.

__This is highly controversial!__ It generates a lot of revenue for companies who use it. But there's a potential dark side: frankly, I think this works so well, because in most cases customers don't understand what they're doing. They click the button, they're buying something and they don't really take the time to read the screen, they just clicked the button because they wanted to get to the thing they bought.

Therefore, you end up with a lot of angry people who say, "I never paid for this, asked for this or bought it." They contact their credit card company and file charge-backs, which causes you problems with your merchant account provider.

To be clear, there are empires that are built on this kind of offer. However, it's also highly controversial and it takes backbone, because you have to hear a lot of negative feedback from customers. Honestly, I don't think it's worth it.

If you **are** going to make this kind of offer, you need to over-communicate to avoid the most serious problems. Make it obvious to people that they are buying a recurring subscription, and how they can cancel their subscription if they want to.

Okay, those are the 9 Types Offers, and the question is…

How do you choose which offer to employ for your particular product or service?

The O.P.E.N. Scale

It comes down to knowing the stages of awareness that your audience happens to be in. I call it "opening the sale." O.P.E.N. is my acronym describing the difference stages of buying awareness.

What does the OPEN acronym stand for? How does it help you understand the stages of awareness of your prospects? It's quite simple:

Oblivious – These are the people who do not know there is a problem. They don't know they have a problem, and they don't know that you exist with a solution. These are the hardest people to sell to.

Pondering – Let's say that you sell a headache remedy and the oblivious person has no headache, has never had a headache and has never thought about buying headache medicine — they're oblivious. The *pondering* person, on the other hand, is beginning to feel the first little twinges of a headache coming on, and they're beginning to ponder where they might get some Tylenol.

Engaged – The *engaged* person now actually *has* a headache. It's not severe and they could probably make it through their day if it didn't get any worse, but they're now actively looking for something to solve this headache problem, before it gets any worse.

Need – This is the person who's in agony, the person with a migraine. Their head feels as though it's splitting open, and they will take *anything* if you say it will solve their headache problem. You don't have to *sell it* or *pitch it* to them. All you need to communicate is that you have a solution. These are the easiest people to sell to.

The secret is to address each of these levels of awareness with a *different* kind of offer; the Oblivious with something like a Soft Offer, while the person in Need probably only requires a simple Hard Offer.

POWER MOVES FOR MORE COMPELLING OFFERS

Power move #1 - Make sure you're selling them what they want

I know this sounds elementary, but it's often overlooked. Make sure you know what they want and sell them exactly what they want. Now you may be thinking, "What they want isn't what they need. They want one thing and they need another."

Even so. You *sell* them what they want and you also *give* them what they *need*.

I like to think of this as "pill treat" copy. If you have a dog you may be familiar with pill treats. They are these weird little gelatinous balls of goo that dogs love to eat. If you have to give your dog a vitamin or some type of medicine, and you try to stick the pill in their mouth, they'll spit it out. They won't eat it from your hand, because it tastes bad to them, just like it would to you or me. So you put that pill inside the pill treat with the goo, and they'll snarf it right up.

Your copy should work the same way. You're going to put the pill inside the "pill treat" and it's more palatable to your audience. Then, you sell them what they want and in the meantime you deliver what they need. But, if you don't sell them what they *want* — they'll never buy. People don't buy based on need or prevention, as a general rule. They buy based on what they want.

No matter what they may tell you or how logical they say they are, it's been proven that even corporate jets are bought for emotional reasons. There'll be plenty of rationale later on to explain *why* it's a good decision, *why* they chose the one they did, but the fact is they decided with their emotions first and they justified with rationale later.

Power move #2 – Make your copy crystal clear

This is not as obvious or as easy as it seems. You have to make sure there's no vagary in your copy, no "voodoo copy." If you can read a paragraph and not be sure of what it said, or if you read it to someone and they aren't sure what it says either, that's "voodoo copy." In fact, what I recommend is that after you've written your offer out, you read it out loud to another human. Only if they can understand it, and repeat the offer back to you in their own words, can you feel confident that it's clear enough.

Power move #3 - Use tipping point bonuses

This has probably worked on *you*. You've probably been contemplating buying some product, service or training program and you couldn't quite make up your mind until you saw one particular bonus they offered and you said all right, if they're going to offer that then I'm going to buy.

You need to pay special attention to the bonuses you offer. People overlook this and treat their bonuses as a second thought. That's a mistake. Spend as much time on your bonuses as you do on any other part of your product creation, and as much time on the copy for the bonus as you do on any other copy that you write. The bonus needs to be as good as or better than what you're selling.

The right kind of bonus is relevant to the product and it enhances the value of the product and makes it even more valuable or easier to use.

CHAPTER 9 QUICK SUMMARY

The 9 Kinds of Offers

OFFER #1 – Hard offer. This doesn't mean it's difficult, it simply means it's straightforward and there are no fuzzy edges. This is what you get.

OFFER #2 – Soft offer. This is the kind of offer that usually involves language like, "Send no money now. We'll send you the kit, shirt, glasses (or whatever) for you to try for 30 days and if you like it we'll automatically charge bill you."

OFFER #3 – Charter offer. This should look familiar to you because you've seen it many times before. It's the first time ever that a product is being offered, and so it's offered at a charter price or rate that nobody will ever get again in the future.

OFFER #4 – Limited supply offer. This just means there are a specific number of available units or positions.

OFFER #5 – Limited time offer. This sounds similar to offer #4, but it's a little different because it's not about the units or positions in the class, it's good for a specific limited time period.

OFFER #6 – The application offer. This is an elite offer. You make people apply for the privilege of buying your product. (Don't laugh this works like crazy).

OFFER #7 – The payment plan offer. This makes it easier to sell higher ticket items because people don't have to pay all at once up front.

OFFER #8 – The one-time offer. You've probably seen this before, it's usually an upsell or add-on sale.

OFFER #9 – The negative option offer. It's also known as forced continuity. This is where people buy something and they get a subscription that goes along with the thing they bought.

THE SECRETS OF
PRODUCT LAUNCH COPY

"Oh yeah, one more thing..."
—Steve Jobs
...on "launch day" every year, just before he unveiled
the one thing everyone really wanted to hear about
(OS X, iPod, iPod video, iPhone, etc.)

The quote starting off this chapter is one of my favorite examples of a product launch.

It's from the late Steve Jobs of Apple.

On launch day every year at the big Apple announcement, Steve Jobs made his keynote presentation about the company, then he announced the exciting new product(s) last.

At the end of his annual public presentation, when he had apparently finished and was preparing to end his talk, he always said, "Oh, and one more thing..."

It may have been OS X, or it might be the iPod, iPod video, or the iPhone, but Steve became known for uttering those words every year, just before he unveiled the one thing everybody really came to hear about.

WHAT IS A PRODUCT LAUNCH?

When you have a sale, or a promotion for your product, you make a special effort to sell it, and you do so by telling stories about it. Those three particular activities—launches, promotions, and story selling—are inextricably intertwined in my mind. I don't think you can separate the three.

Any time you do a promotion, you're doing a miniature launch.

The first thing you need to do is decide what kind of launch or product roll-out you're going to do. Will it be a full launch, one that's going to last over a period of several weeks from beginning to end? Are you going to do a *compressed* launch, which might be a process of launching your product over a week to ten days, or are you going to do *a mini-launch*, which could be more like a promotion that takes place over one to three days?

When we talk about the time frame these launches need, it's important to keep in mind that a product launch consists of a sequence of marketing events that form a story. There's something very powerful at work here, and that is the need for the human mind to close open loops.

The incomplete loop in your mind draws and magnetizes your attention, so when you have a sequence of marketing events—for instance, a sequence of e-mails, pieces of sales copy, blog posts, PDF reports, videos, and audios—there is a need in the human psyche to complete the sequence, to finish the story.

Your next step is to "map out" your launch. Plan it on a calendar, even if you're doing just a promotion, not a "full" launch. Think of it like a launch, and at the very least, map out the beginning, middle, and end on the calendar. That will give you a framework to plan your promotion and make it more effective.

If you're marketing on the internet, you're *always* doing a product launch. The only question is, are you doing it well or doing it poorly? Consciously or unconsciously? Your copy, your website, your videos, each of these elements is telling a story. Whether you're consciously directing that story and deciding how you want it to affect your readers or viewers, is up to you.

If you let it happen unconsciously, you may not be happy with the results. If you consciously direct the story and think about the strategy behind it… if you make the tactics fit the strategy… then you can improve your results in almost every case.

A BEGINNER'S GUIDE TO PRODUCT LAUNCHES

For a full treatment of product launches, I recommend the book *Launch!* by Jeff Walker. The book is a fun and comprehensive read about the subject. Jeff pioneered the concept of the online product launch, and teaches the full process in an online learning program called *Product Launch Formula*.

Meanwhile, here's a beginner's guide to product launches.

PRODUCT LAUNCH USES PSYCHOLOGICAL "TRIGGERS"

Product launches work because they employ all the psychological triggers of influence. This subject was examined in detail by Dr. Robert Cialdini in his book, *Influence*.

Influence is the result of university peer-reviewed studies demonstrating the factors that influence people's behavior. Employing these psychological triggers is what makes the launch process so powerful. The triggers Dr. Cialdini identified are:

- **Reciprocity.** We feel if someone gives us something, we need to give them something in return. Thus, if you give your prospects valuable free videos or information, they will be more inclined to buy from you.

- **Commitment & Consistency.** People will take great pains to make their actions match their words or previous commitments (even small ones like signing up for your email newsletter.)
- **Liking.** We tend to buy from people we feel an emotional connection to – people we like. This is why personality marketing is so powerful.
- **Authority**. People are hard-wired to obey authority – or even the mere appearance of authority. This is why credibility, celebrity endorsements, and symbols of authority (white lab coats, police uniforms, and the cleric's collar) evoke such strong emotional responses from us.
- **Social Proof.** This is connected to the principle of liking. We look at others to see how they are responding, searching for clues as to how we should respond. Have you won awards, or been featured in big media? Show it off.
- **Scarcity.** This is perhaps the most familiar aspect of launches. "Scarcity" or "urgency." People are more motivated by feeling they're about to miss out on something than they are by the thought of that same something might benefit them. In other words, tell people that can't have it, and they want it even more. Time-limited prices, restricted quantities, and qualification requirements all work to create a feeling of scarcity and prompt people to buy.

Product launches do not, as has been suggested, make the sales letter irrelevant. In fact, more copy is required for a launch than for normal sales processes. A launch distributes the sales letter over several forms of media, and over a longer period of time. But the fact is, the entire launch is copy. There's a *lot* of copy required when doing a product launch, which leads us to…

LAUNCH COPY BEGINS LONG BEFORE THE SALES LETTER

In fact, the sales letter, even though it might be sizable (some recent launches have used fifty-page sales letters!), may only represent 10–20 percent of the actual copy used in the product launch. This includes:

- Blog posts, e-mails, surveys, and articles.
- Copy that's written to recruit partners.
- Copy that your partners can send out to their lists to help launch your product.
- There is an entire sequence of e-mails, both before and after the launch.
- The actual sales letter itself.
- Follow-up e-mail.

Launch copy is *not* irrelevant. To the contrary, launch copy is crucial, and is part of a sequence. All the psychological factors implemented in the various discreet copy elements put the potential buyers into a more receptive frame of mind. When they finally see the sales letter, they're more likely to be influenced to buy. In fact, they may have already made their decision to buy, and are just looking for a "Buy Now" button to push.

PRODUCT LAUNCHES ARE FIRST A STORY

The most effective way to set the launch up for success is to do so by making it into a story. The story might be as simple as, "I had a problem, and I figured out a way to solve it. Now, I would like to share with you how I solved that problem."

If you do nothing but write a bunch of blatant hard-hammering sales messages, you're not going to have much of a launch, because people need a story to engage them emotionally.

KNOW THE ARC OF YOUR STORY

We will spend more time on how you develop your story later.

For the purposes of this discussion, just remember that your product launch *is* a story, and there must be an *arc* to your story at its simplest level.

A story has a *beginning*, a *middle*, and an *end*. Your launch needs to have the same thing: a feeling of resolution at the end. In that moment of resolution at the end of your launch, you also want to leave people wanting more. That is why they buy.

STORYBOARD YOUR LAUNCH ON A CALENDAR

Keep yourself on track during your launch by having a plan that's disciplined by dates. Some of you might be thinking: "Ray, I'm not real sure what the elements of my story need to be, so how will I know how to put that on a calendar?"

Let me walk you through a thumbnail sketch scenario of what your launch might be like. Let's say you're launching a product that's about how to house-train your dog. You've figured out a miracle method for house-training a dog that only takes two or three days.

This is something a lot of pet owners would love to know about. They want to hear your story. They want to hear how you discovered this method. They want to hear how you bought your new pet and how that pet had house-training problems and how you were desperately searching for a solution.

Your launch process could start with something as simple as putting up a blog or perhaps going to forums where pet owners hang out and putting up a post that says, "I'm working on putting together a report on how to house-train your dog; do you guys have any suggestions about that?"

Take some of those answers and begin to form the basis of your launch. Maybe you blog about some of the struggles that you had with training your dog. Then a few days later, you begin posting about how you've discovered a method that seems to be working.

Just make sure it's all true. *Your stories should always be true. I* hope that goes without saying. Do not tell lies. You're better than that, and don't need to do it. You can always find a *real* story.

If you didn't have the experience of discovering the method that allowed you to teach your dog to not soil the carpet in three days, but instead you acquired the rights to a product that teaches people how to do that, what's the story there? How about this: "I have a dog that kept having accidents in the house, so I found this product that taught me how to fix the problem and it did, so I bought the rights to the product."

That's a darn good story. In fact, you've heard that story in a famous marketing campaign. It wasn't about dog training; it was about electric shavers. Remember Victor Kiam and the Remington company? "I liked this razor so much, I bought the company."

Map out on a calendar when you're going to release these pieces of the story. Then set a date and tell the people on your mailing list, who follow you on social media, who read your blog or who read in those forums you frequented, that on May 23rd you're going to open the doors and have fifty copies to sell of this book you've had printed, along with the DVD. If they want one, they need to get on the waiting list and be ready to go.

Then you update your list on your progress, perhaps by sending them an e-mail to let them know, "Now we have one hundred people on the waiting list, so it's important when we open the doors on the 23rd that you move quickly and buy your copy." Once it's sold out, you send them another message, make another blog post, and make up your sales letter describing the product.

You can begin to see how these represent points on a calendar. Laying these points out on the calendar is what I mean by "storyboarding" your launch.

CAST YOUR STORY

Who are the players? I want you to think about this carefully, because you need to think through who the viewers of your story might be, who the potential customers or prospects are, and who the players in your story are.

For instance, if you want your joint venture partners to send an e-mail to their list telling their subscribers about your product or service, you're going to need to write copy that persuades them to do that.

You'll need a story for your present subscribers, your list members, and a story for new customers, prospects, partners, and the marketing community in general. Remember, they're observing the process of your launch to see how well it goes—to observe your skill as a marketer.

11 LAUNCH COPY COMPONENTS

Here are the minimum required pieces of copy for a proper product launch.

1) List-building copy.

This is where you're writing copy that starts building a list, perhaps using a blog or commenting in a forum.

One way to do this is, setting up a landing page, then making posts to your blog that talk about the fact that you're conducting a survey for a book you're thinking about writing or for some articles you want to create.

If it's in a community where a lot of activity and communication takes place naturally, then it could just be as simple as saying, "I'm taking a survey of iguana owners. What are the biggest problems you face as an iguana owner? What are the best things about owning an iguana? What are your funniest iguana stories?" I know I'm picking a ridiculous market as an illustration, but this idea will work in any market.

Then you need copy for your squeeze page. You need copy for your confirmation e-mail. You need copy for your follow-up e-mail, and you're going to need to think about how that continues to tell your story.

2) Survey copy.
As your list and traffic grow, you want to start asking your market what bugs them. Find out what their pain is.

There are two ways to go about this when you're thinking about how you're going to create and market your product. You can focus on relieving a certain pain in the life of the prospect or you can focus on moving the prospect towards some type of pleasurable outcome.

People will respond more readily and will do more to get out of pain than to get into pleasure. I tend to want to focus on the pain-relieving aspects of the product or service.

You could just as easily focus on the pleasure-inducing aspect. That would be good in hobby markets, for instance, such as the model train market. People do model train activities because those activities make them feel good, not because they relieve some great deep psychological pain. That's a choice you are going to want to make. I recommend focusing on finding their pain and ways to relieve it.

3) Product.
This is especially important if you're creating an information product. You want to think of your product itself as copy because it's making

a continual sale to your buyer. The sale it's making is, "I was worth investing in. I am giving you value."

You need to think in terms of how you structure the product, how it is written in language that reaffirms the decision the prospect made when he or she decided to invest in it. Make sure it addresses the questions and points that were in the copy that sold it to begin with. How many times have you purchased an information product and after you bought it, read it, listened to it, or watched the videos wondered, "What happened to those bullet points that made me buy this? I don't even see where those are answered."

You want to make sure you address those in the product itself. Think of the product as an extension of your copy.

4) JV recruitment copy.

This is joint venture recruitment copy. When you're performing a launch, you don't want to rely on just your own list. What if you don't have a list; you're starting from scratch, and you need to create a list from nothing?

The way you do that is with joint venture partners. Let's say, for instance, you are a veterinary doctor and you created a product on treating your pet for common ailments at home: "How to do preventative health care with your pet at home and how to use holistic remedies for your pet to save money and have a healthier pet."

Let's say you created this product, and you have good information, but you have no list. This very situation was faced by my coaching and copywriting client Dr. Andrew Jones. He created the product I just spoke of and did over $44,000 in his first week, creating an on-going income stream based on this product with no e-mail list.

How did he do this? He got joint venture partners. He called other vendors who offered products to the market he wanted to speak to: pet owners who care about their pets. He said to them, "I'm going to have this product. If you will send an e-mail to the folks on your e-mail list, and they buy from your e-mail, then I will give you half of the proceeds from that sale."

If you're familiar with the world of online marketing, this doesn't seem like such a novel idea. However, the people Dr. Andrew spoke with had *never* heard of this kind of deal before. Outside of the internet marketing world, this is news – and usually, you will find people who are thrilled to partner with you.

5) Pre-launch copy.
The next few components are all part of this. Here is where you begin building anticipation, scarcity, and social proof. Get your market as excited about your launch as you are.

6) The "Big PDF."
This is where you're going to write a white paper, a position paper or special report that spells out your platform or USP (unique selling proposition). It needs to really grab people's attention.

It might be a collection of advice from well-known experts in your industry, with you as the publisher and editor. It might be an e-book or procedure manual that you authored yourself.

Whatever you choose to publish, it's important that it is appealing to your audience; that they will want it enough to pay for it, if necessary.

7) Unpredictable plot complication copy.
We're borrowing language from television and movie script writers now. "Unpredictable plot complications" means things will occur you didn't plan for. Some people identify them as problems; I like to identify them as storytelling opportunities.

Let's say your server goes down. That's the one that people know most commonly. "Wow! We had so much traffic from people who wanted to get a copy of our big PDF that our server went down."

That's a story, but it's a story that's been told so, it might have lost some of its effectiveness. Even if the proverbial "server crash" really does happen to you, it might be better to look for a different story.

Maybe you got a nasty e-mail from someone who doesn't like the way you're promoting your product or offer. Share that with the people on your pre-launch list and let them see the story unfold. I promise you, if you do that, you'll win the hearts of the people on your list. Your prospects will leap to your defense. (I know because it happened to me during my own launch.)

Again, make certain your stories are *true*—be open to them, and I promise you they will occur. A product launch is such a complex endeavor, things will happen. Things will go wrong; unexpected things will occur. It's not always a problem; sometimes it's a great opportunity.

You might get an unexpected phone call from Tony Robbins' office and he says to you, "I need you to come speak at the Learning Annex; we're having a big event, and I've heard about your products. I would love to have you on the stage at the same time as me, so you can speak about whatever it is you teach."

Wouldn't that be a story worth telling? Yes, it's exaggerated. Yes, it's dramatic. But it actually did happen to one of my clients! Those kinds of stories make for great storytelling opportunities during your product launch.

8) Countdown copy.

This is where we start playing on the anticipation and scarcity. Again, this is taking a leaf from the book by Robert Cialdini. We're letting people know, "On this date, you will be able to buy tickets to this workshop. You'll be able to buy one of the kits for our product that teaches you how to have a better relationship, but we've only had 100 printed! You will need to be ready when the countdown reaches zero on date (x) at time (x)."

Countdown copy is very effective. Yes, you've seen it done in the marketing world. I know it still works in internet marketing, and it works even better in markets outside the marketing world, so make sure you include countdown copy as one of your copy components in your launch.

9) *The sales letter.*

You knew we had to get to this sooner or later! A carefully crafted sales letter is key to the success of your launch. There have been a couple stupendously successful online product launches over the last year. Controversy arose over the sales letter.

On one side of the controversy, people said, "Wow, Copywriter X must be great. He wrote a letter for that product launch and brought in a million dollars in a single day!" (In one case, a million dollars in less than an hour.)

On the other side of the controversy, people said, "The sales letter was irrelevant. You could have just put a 'Buy Now' button on that page and people would have bought. You didn't need a sales letter; it had nothing to do with it."

What's the truth?

Are sales letters irrelevant in the face of product launches? I don't believe so.

Every form of communication used during your launch is sales copy, and is part of the "sales letter." In fact, you can think of a product launch as one giant sales letter, just broken into smaller pieces and distributed over time in different media (text, audio, email, video, info-graphics, etc.)

Even if a buyer never sees your actual sales letter — they are still sold by it.

What about launches that use only a video and no written sales copy at all? The script of the video is the sales letter. And just for the record, failing to also supply a written version of the sales letter for people whose preferred form of learning is through the written word is a huge mistake.

Finally, the messaging you create in a well-crafted sales letter informs and shapes all of your communications with your prospects. Even if a buyer never sees your actual sales letter – they are still sold by it.

10) Post-launch-week copy.

As much as 30 percent of your sales may come in the week after your big launch day. Think about that. If you don't do any post-launch e-mails, blog posts, or marketing activities, if you don't have any post-launch e-mails for your joint venture partners or affiliates to send out, then you're leaving loads of money on the table. You need to make sure those e-mails are carefully crafted, planned, and ready to go.

11) The missing piece.

I see this component left out all the time: following up with your buyers and prospects to make your launch become a profitable business.

Often during the process of a launch, a marketer builds a list of potential buyers, then stops marketing after the big launch day, or at least after launch week.

If you're in the small percentage of marketers who are savvy enough to continue marketing the week after the launch, the "missing piece" is to continue to follow up with the people on that list, because they were interested in what you had to offer. They were interested in what you had to say.

Continue talking with them, dialoguing with them, and making offers to them. Just because they didn't buy your initial launch offer, it doesn't mean they may not be interested in other things.

PROMOTIONS ARE MINI-LAUNCHES.

If you take the entire process and all the copy components I just outlined and compressed those into a couple of days, you have a promotion, or a mini-launch.

The best promotions are a story. Even a sale, like a back-to-school sale, is a story.

The story is, "Summer's over; the kids need some new clothes for school; they need some school supplies. We're going to put those things on sale to help you out because we know you need the help, so come to our Back-to-School Sale. It's good for a few days only."

There's your scarcity, urgency, and timeline on the calendar. It's a mini-launch.

THE MAGIC POWER OF "STORY SELLING."

Stories are the process by which we learn, live, and believe anything.

I'd like you to think about that carefully and test that statement. Don't just nod your head and say, "Yes, that's good information, Ray." Think it through.

> **Stories are the process by which we learn, live, and believe anything.**

Try to think of something you've learned and lived through, something that you believe, that is *not* expressed as a story.

I don't think you can. In the next chapter, in fact, we will take a look at how Hollywood tells and sells its stories, and how we can borrow some of their ideas for marketing campaigns.

PRODUCT LAUNCHES ARE A TEAM SPORT

Product launches are a team sport. There is a false perception that you can sit in your basement at home, dream up a product, type it out, create it on your computer, get online and find your JV partners, launch it, and do it all by yourself.

First of all, if you have JV partners or affiliates, *you're not doing it by yourself.*

Secondly, the most successful product launches involve a number of minds working actively together, sculpting and crafting the launch as it progresses. If you keep this in mind and involve other people in what you're doing, you'll find your launch to be much more successful.

CHAPTER 10 QUICK SUMMARY

The Secrets of Product Launch Copy

Product Launch Copy Uses Psychological "Triggers." These triggers of influence were identified by Dr. Robert Cialdini in his book, Influence. They are:

- Reciprocity
- Commitment & Consistency
- Liking
- Authority
- Social Proof
- Scarcity

Launch Copy Begins Long Before the Sales Letter. The sales letter may be only 10–20 percent of the actual copy for the launch.

Product Launches Are First ... a Story. The most effective way to set the context for a launch is through a story.

11 Components of Successful Product Launch Copy

1. **List Building.** Write copy that starts building a list using a blog.
2. **Survey.** As your list and traffic grow, start asking your market what bugs them; find their pain.
3. **Product.** Think of your product as copy.
4. **JV Recruitment.** Your first sale is to your joint venture partners.
5. **Pre-Launch Copy.** Begin building the feelings of anticipation, scarcity, and social proof.
6. **The "Big PDF."** Write a white paper or special report that spells out your platform or USP.

7. **Unpredictable Plot Complications.** Be ready to tell the story you didn't anticipate.
8. **Countdown Copy.** Use copy to whip your buyers into a buying frenzy.
9. **Sales Letter.** A carefully crafted sales letter is key to the success of your launch.
10. **Post-Launch Week.** As much as 30 percent of your sales may come in the week after launch day.
11. **The Missing Piece.** Follow up with your buyers and prospects to make your launch into a business.

---

*Claim **your FREE membership** (retail value $197) including a growing library of templates & tutorials, visit CopyThatSellsBook.com (no credit card required).*

11

THE SECRETS OF WRITING BLOCKBUSTER COPY BY WATCHING MOVIES

"Those who tell the stories rule the world."
—Hopi Native American proverb

In the course of writing some blockbuster promotions (a number of my sales letters have brought in seven-figure paydays for my clients). I've seen what works when it comes to copy.

I've also written some promotions that did not work so well on the first run. It pains me to admit that – and these cases are few and far between – but that's the unvarnished truth.

Comparing the many successful pieces of copy I've written, I've identified what I believe is the single biggest difference between copy that rocks (i.e., converts like crazy) and copy that sucks.

I believe that you can inject this one element into any anemic, pathetic, lackluster piece of copy… and transform that underperforming sales letter into an order-getting engine of prosperity.

How did I stumble upon this "secret"?

Watching movies.

More specifically, watching movie *trailers.*

WHAT MAKES A BLOCKBUSTER MOVIE TRAILER?

Of course, you and I know that not all the movies live up to the trailer. We've all had that experience of seeing the actual film and saying, "Well, they put all the *best* parts in the previews."

So, just for the moment, let's think of your product as the movie. And let's think of your sales copy as the "trailer." And just for now, let's assume your product or offer lives up to the promise of the trailer.

So, nobody's going to see the movie – or buy your product – and then want their money back. Nobody's going to say, "The best parts were in the previews."

Can we agree to that, oh Constant Marketer?

Okay. Then the question becomes… how do we create a "trailer" – in our case, a sales letter – that makes people decide on the spot that they must have the actual product?

The secret of great movie trailers – and of great sales copy – is something I call the Dominant Story Idea, or "DSI" for short.

HOW THE DSI TRANSFORMS COPY FROM BORING TO BLOCKBUSTER

I'm going to give you an example of how this whole "DSI" thing can actually save your bacon, and turn a losing sales letter into a winner (in just a few minutes).

The best and most successful movie trailers do three things without fail:

- Give you the Dominant Story Idea (DSI)
- Offer a sample of the feelings you'll get from the movie itself
- Provide proof that the movie "works"

Want proof? No problem.

I've selected a couple of example movie trailers, and we'll assume you saw the trailer or a TV commercial for the movies we're discussing. If you really want to see them for yourself, a brief visit to YouTube will get you the trailers in question. I've purposely chosen older movies to avoid spoiling a film for you if you haven't seen it yet.

Our first example is for the movie *21*, starring Kevin Spacey.

1. **Dominant Story Idea:** college math whiz uses his skills to beat the Vegas casinos… gets seduced by the dark side, and gets into trouble with some very bad guys.
2. **Sample feelings:** we see Ben Campbell in his innocent phase… we see him winning… we see him getting seduced by money, power, and very hot women… and then we see him getting into some really scary trouble. Will he prevail?
3. **Proof the movie "works:"** we're shown Kevin Spacey, Kathe Bosworth and Laurence Fishburn (proven actors we love)… some very compelling scenes (tightly edited)… and in the background we're anchored by the sound of the Doors singing "Break on Through to the Other Side"

Our second example is, incidentally, just about the same story – but this movie comes from even further back on the calendar (1993). It's *The Firm*, based on John Grisham's book. I chose it to make a point: you don't have to come up with a new idea to have a hit. You just need to tell the story in a fresh way.

Here's a summary of *The Firm*, starring Tom Cruise.

1. **Dominant Story Idea:** young lawyer passes the bar and gets a dream job – with great pay and even a free BMW. Seems too good to be true. In fact, it is: he's working for the Mob. And if he wants out, they're going to kill him.

2. **Sample feelings:** we see Mitch McDeer in his innocent phase... we see him winning the new job, the car, and the status he so desperately wants... we see him getting seduced by money, power, and very hot women... and then we see him getting into some really scary trouble. Will he prevail? (Hmm. Sounds familiar.)

3. **Proof the movie "works:"** overtly, we're shown Tom Cruise, Gene Hackman, and Hal Holbrook (proven actors we love)... some very compelling scenes (tightly edited)... and in the background we're anchored by the sound of the suspenseful and ominous music (hinting that bad things are about to happen to dear Mitch McDeer).

Back to my point: how this applies to your copy.

USING THE DSI TO CREATE WINNING SALES COPY

Well, it should be getting clear for you by now... you need to do these same three things with your copy.

As long as your product actually solves a problem, this formula will work for you.

All you need to do is the following:

1. **Showcase Your Dominant Story Idea:** Imagine you're making a Hollywood Movie Trailer... how would you sum up your DSI? Look at the movie examples above for some clues.

2. **Sample feelings:** Again, looking to our movie trailer examples, can you show – in your copy – some scenes that will help the reader feel the feelings they want to get from your product? You do this by telling stories, and directing the reader's imagination so that they see themselves in the end state your product provides (financial freedom, quitting their job, being

a best-selling author, enjoying their new car, or whatever your product does for them). And here's a key: they must link this end state to your product. Let me be clear: by the time they're done with your copy, they need to see that the only way they can reasonably expect to get to that end state is… by using your product.

3. **Proof the product "works:"** you do this in the ways we're familiar with: testimonials, case studies, before-and-after photo and video, screenshots, etc. Showing "celebrity" endorsements will improve your results by multitudes. Just remember you don't need Kevin Spacey or Tom Cruise… chances are your niche has its own celebrities that will work just as well (or even better) for your purposes.

So how does this work in actual practice?

PUTTING THE DSI TO WORK IN YOUR OWN COPY… TODAY

You might be tempted to say, "That's great for Hollywood, Ray, but how does it work for me? I just want to juice up my sales letter and get some sales of my product… which has nothing to do with movies!"

No problem.

Let me give you an action plan for using the DSI method in your marketing. And you can start immediately – as in, today.

First, you need to identify the three elements used by movie studios to "sell" their movies to the public. So, thinking in terms of your own product:

1. **What's the Dominant Story Idea of your sales copy?** *(E.g., "Weird exercise routine provides world's best workout in just 4 minutes," or "Collapsing financial markets have produced an overlooked opportunity for investors" etc.)*

2. **What are three ways you can provide Sample Feelings for your readers... so they picture themselves using your product and enjoying its benefits?** *(E.g., Can you tell them a True But Amazing Story? Show them a brief video? Let them try one of your techniques?)*

3. **What are three powerful ways you can Prove Your Product Works?** *(E.g., Celebrity endorsements, before-and-after, well-known examples, etc.)*

Once you've actually written these things down, your next task is to incorporate them into your copy. How do you do that? Simple.

Get the DSI into your headline and lead.

This might mean you have to ditch that worn out "Who Else" headline... but are you really going to cry about that? For instance, in one of the examples above, I could actually just use my DSI as the headline:

World's Best Workout... In Just 4 Minutes

Next, summarize your Sample Feelings elements and place them in the Deck Copy (right under the headline). Bullet points work best here. To continue using our exercise example, I might write:

In this Special Report, you will learn the amazing (but true) story behind the world's fastest workout. You'll discover:

- *How this method of "fast exercise" was discovered, and how scientific testing has proven it to be effective.*
- *The "miracle transformation" that took the method's inventor from 300 pounds to 160... lowered his blood pressure... and took 30 years off his biological age (and how you can do the same — or better).*

- *__The principles behind the 4 minute workout__ and how you can start using them right now to build your strength and endurance.*

BUT... HOW DO I FIND MY DSI?

I've actually left the most important question until the end.

If you've looked at your product and decided that you just don't know what makes it different from any other... don't despair. I can show you *why* you need not despair with a simple exercise: can you name the following movie?

Young man discovers he is destined for greater things, is taken under the wing of a wise older man, and must undertake a challenging quest to fulfill his destiny. He passes through many grueling trials, but in the end triumphs over the forces of evil and wins the day.

Hmmm.

Star Wars?
The Lord of the Rings?
Batman Begins?
Superman?
Karate Kid?

The answer is... any or all of the above. And hundreds of other movies as well. While they are each, in essence, the same story....they are also each unique. They are "the same but different".

So how do you find your *own* unique DSI?

This is the part I can't put into a formula for you – you've got to do the work yourself. But here are some tips that will help you...

- Immerse yourself in your own product. Know it inside and out.
- Read copy from other markets (different products entirely) and ask, "How MIGHT this story apply to my own product?"

- Watch the news. What are the top stories and how could they be tied to your promotion?
- Ask yourself this question… if your product were a movie, what movie would it be? And then see if you can "theme" your product around that idea. Roy Williams, a radio advertising expert, thought of himself as something like the "Wizard of Oz"… and in a flash of insight branded himself as "The Wizard of Ads." Can you do something similar with your product or service?

WHAT TO DO NOW

If you can find your own Dominant Story Idea, and build your sales copy around it, you'll almost certainly increase your sales and profits. Because I can promise you – your competition is almost certainly not doing any of this.

Look, it's not just me saying it.

David Ogilvy, arguably one of the greatest ad writers who ever lived, said this:

"Unless your advertising contains a Big Idea, it will pass like a ship in the night. I doubt if more than one campaign in a hundred contains a Big Idea."

Now you know what will set your campaign (or sales letter, or product launch) apart from all the others: it's your DSI.

Spend some time identifying it and incorporating it into your copy.

The results will be your reward!

CHAPTER 11 QUICK SUMMARY

How the DSI Transforms Copy from Boring to Blockbuster

The best and most successful movie trailers do three things without fail:

1. Give you the Dominant Story Idea (DSI)
2. Offer a sample of the feelings you'll get from the movie itself
3. Provide proof that the movie "works"

Putting the DSI to Work in Your Own Copy

First, you need to identify the same three elements used by movie studios to "sell" their movies to the public. So, thinking in terms of your own product:

1. **What's the Dominant Story Idea of your sales copy?** *(E.g., "Weird exercise routine provides world's best workout in just 4 minutes," or "Collapsing financial markets have produced an overlooked opportunity for investors," etc.)*

2. **What are three ways you can provide Sample Feelings for your readers... so they picture themselves using your product and enjoying its benefits?** *(E.g., Can you tell them a True But Amazing Story? Show them a brief video? Let them try one of your techniques?)*

3. **What are three powerful ways you can Prove Your Product Works?** *(E.g., Celebrity endorsements, before-and-after, well-known examples, etc.)*

---

*Claim **your FREE membership** (retail value $197) including a growing library of templates & tutorials, visit CopyThatSellsBook.com (no credit card required).*

12

THE COPYWRITING CHALLENGE

When all is said and done, there's only one way to get really good at writing sales copy – and that's by writing lots of copy, putting it in front of readers, and noticing their reaction.

The reaction you're looking for is the *buying* reaction.

You'll know your copy is working through that most thrilling kind of evidence: people decide to give you their money because of the words you wrote.

Now that you've read this book, and seen first-hand some of my very best money-getting copy techniques, you probably can't wait to publish your copy and see what happens.

Perhaps you already have – *bravo!*

In fact, I'd like to issue my signature two-part challenge to you.

CHALLENGE PART ONE

Take *one* idea from this book and start the implementation of that idea in the next 2 minutes. Obviously, you'll have to pick something that *can* be started in 2 minutes. But don't get too caught up in *completing* this task, just get it started.

That could possibly look like:

- Sending an email to a customer.
- Writing a few new subject lines or headlines.
- Jotting down some ideas for a new autoresponder series.
- Or even scheduling a brainstorming session on new copywriting projects.

There are a limitless number of possibilities. Just pick *one* and then do it.

It's that simple.

CHALLENGE PART TWO

The next challenge is a little more involved, but the potential payoff is huge.

Take some time (perhaps in that brainstorming session you just scheduled) to outline a new offer and the basic concepts of the sales copy for that offer. Then schedule time on your calendar to get this new sales letter written.

Pick the "money-getting date" on the calendar – a date no more than 30 days from today – the date on which you will publish that new sales letter and begin promoting it.

Then, no matter what, stick to that schedule!

If you do this, 30 days from now you may find your business has been revolutionized for the better.

You might even have written the sales letter that turns your business, and even your **life** completely around.

Okay, I've issued the challenges.

Do you accept? *Good.*

Get to work!

ABOUT THE AUTHOR

Ray Edwards is one of the world's highest-paid advertising copywriters and marketing/business coaches.

His sales copy and marketing advice are amazingly effective – having sold an estimated $100 million in products and services.

Ray's all-star list of clients includes *New York Times* best-selling authors Tony Robbins *(Awaken the Giant Within, MONEY Master the Game)*, Jack Canfield, and Mark Victor Hansen (co-creators *of Chicken Soup for the Soul)*, Joel Comm (author of *Twitter Power, Ka-Ching,* and *The Adsense Code*), Robert Allen (author of *Nothing Down* and *Creating Wealth*), and Raymond Aaron (author of *Double Your Income Doing What You Love*).

Ray has written thousands of pages of copy — radio commercials, TV commercials, direct mail pieces, one-sheets, fliers, brochures, billboards, music on-hold scripts, training manuals, corporate policy and procedures, website copy, and email marketing campaigns.

He speaks frequently at seminars on copywriting, promotions, and marketing for professionals in those fields. He has appeared in magazines, newspapers, trade journals, and on national radio and TV.

For more resources, a weekly internet radio show (podcast), and to subscribe to Ray's FREE email newsletter, visit RayEdwards.com

HOW TO CONTACT RAY

If you are interested in online business, marketing, copywriting, and how to be a follower of Jesus in the marketplace, Ray can help.

For more information about keynotes and workshops, contact Ray Edwards International, Inc.:

Phone: (509) 624–2220
Email: info@RayEdwards.com
Online: www.RayEdwards.com

Ray Edwards International, Inc.
2910 E 57th Ave Ste. 5 #330
Spokane, WA 99223

Sign-up for Ray Edwards' email newsletter at:
www.RayEdwards.com

To purchase bulk copies of this book at a discount for your customers, or for your organization, please contact Ray Edwards International, Inc.:
specialsales@RayEdwards.com or (509) 624–2220

FREE MEMBERSHIP FOR READERS OF
HOW TO WRITE COPY THAT SELLS

Retail Value of $197

Claim Your FREE Templates & Training Membership ...

- The **1 Hour Copywriting Template** and Guide.
- The **Copywriting Quick-Start Training** (secret tactics for speed copywriting).
- The **one-page copywriting guide** (the basics of copywriting "at-a-glance").

... and so much more! Claim your free training now.
CopyThatSellsBook.com

9 781614 485025